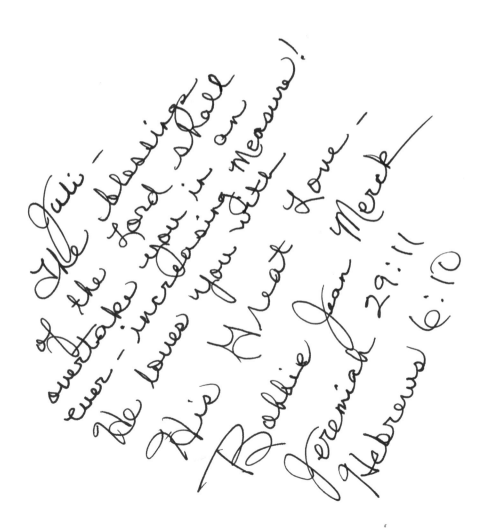

Juli —

The blessings
of the Lord shall
overtake you in an
ever - increasing Measure)!
He loves you with
His Great Love -

Bobbie Jean Merck
Jeremiah 29:11
Hebrews 6:10

Ask of Me

A JOURNEY IN THE ESSENCE OF INTERCESSORY PRAYER

BOBBIE JEAN MERCK

insight
PUBLISHING GROUP
Tulsa, Oklahoma

ASK OF ME
© 2008 by Bobbie Jean Merck

Published by Insight Publishing Group
8801 S. Yale, Suite 410
Tulsa, OK 74137
918-493-1718

Unless otherwise noted, all Scripture quotations are taken from the Holy Bible: *King James Version.* Scripture quotations marked AMP are taken from *The Amplified Bible*, Old Testament, © 1965, 1987 by Zondervan Corporation. New Testament, © 1958, 1987 by The Lockman Foundation. Used by permission. Scripture quotations marked NLT are taken from the Holy Bible, New Living Translation, © 1996, 2004. Used by permission of Tyndale House Publishers, Inc., Wheaton, Illinois 60189. All rights reserved.

ISBN: 1-932503-74-9
ISBN: 978-1-932503-74-6

Library of Congress catalog card number: 2008922605

Printed in the United States of America

Dedication

To Sarah G. Payne, my mother, affectionately known as "Mama Sarah" by all who know and love her. No words could adequately express the gratitude I have for your love and encouragement for me throughout my life, and your tireless prayer for me and the ministry of A Great Love. Countless and limitless great works to the glory of Almighty God were and still are accomplished in your "prayer house."

Contents

Preface
Acknowledgments

Preface

With so much information in various media formats available, you might be asking yourself, does the Body of Christ really need one more book about how to walk and talk with Jesus? Don't we hear enough preached and prophesied about the art of prayer and having a personal relationship with God? There are volumes of texts that would quench the thirst of the most inquisitive mind. Would the Holy Spirit move upon one of His servants to once again pen teachings to prevail upon His people to seek understanding of the power of intercessory prayer and a deeper spiritual walk? Simply said, "yes."

Each of us has been given a sphere of influence, whether it is the intimacy of family and friends, the local church, or the Body of Christ at large. We tend to keep within circles of familiarity, broadening it as we move on in life, but still limited to our social contacts and circumstances. Given the enormous scope of Christian writings, it would be nearly impossible to read and investigate everything that has been written on any one topic. Consequently, we become selective, listening to those who we believe have exhibited credibility; those who have been tested and proven; those who bring clarity and understanding of God's Word to us. That being the human condition, it seems reasonable that the love of God would prevail upon many voices to speak throughout the ages to minister His truths, grounded in His Word, in order to reach each sphere of influence in every age.

This book adds another voice of understanding of the Word and the Holy Spirit with regard to prayer. It expresses experiences in the supernatural, and reveals adventures with the Lord to inspire the reader in the pursuit of his or her own depth of relationship with God, while fulfilling the plans and purposes He has for His sons and daughters. Our walk with Him is both simple and profound. Both the seen and the unseen universe are at His disposal to respond when His people in obedience and simple faith respond to His call to, "Ask of Me."

> *"Ask of me, and I shall give thee the heathen for thine inheritance, and the uttermost parts of the earth for thy possession" (Psalm 2:8).*

This book reflects the knowledge, wisdom, and revelation I have gleaned from the many years that I have been taught by the Holy Spirit and the Word of God about the ministry of intercession. In the daily hours spent in the presence of Almighty God, He has directed me to bring forth the understanding of intercessory prayer through precept and practice. It is my deepest desire that the life-changing message of this book will bless the Body of Christ and bring people to a closer walk with Jesus for His glory.

Acknowledgments

First and most of all, I must acknowledge **Almighty God** the Father, my Lord and Savior, **Jesus Christ**, and the **Holy Spirit**, through Whom all that is of eternal quality endures. It is *"... in him we live, and move, and have our being..." (Acts 17:28).*

Margaret Gunnels, my great-grandmother, was one of the earliest influences in my life. As a faithful Methodist who zealously worshipped God, she was known to have experienced miracles for herself and others for whom she prayed. I will always be grateful for the ways she touched my life.

Phil Halverson, Jeanne Wilkerson, and **Rachel Teafatiller** were instrumental in the early development in my ministry of and my understanding of intercession. They exemplified integrity and commitment to fulfilling the call of God on their lives in intercessory prayer. Phil and Jeanne are now a part of the great cloud of witnesses in heaven, cheering all of us on to finish our race. The anointing and influence on the lives of those they touched continues.

Jane Johnston, my fellow intercessor and loyal friend, thank you for the innumerable hours over the past decades spent in prayer and intercession for me and the ministry of A Great Love, and specifically your prayers in bringing this book forth. Most importantly, you are a friend of God.

Gene and Bess Porterfield, thank you for your faith in God on behalf of this ministry. Your support for this ministry and for the publishing of this book touches me deeply as it does the heart of God.

Tracey Merck, my daughter-in-law and personal assistant, thank you for the diligent administrative work you have done with excellence and care. Books simply cannot be published without the kind of attention to all of the many details that you have given so freely and lovingly.

Eva Benevento, thank you for your dedication, editorial input, evaluations and suggestions for the text. To God be the glory. Eva, you, Ben, Joshua, and Hannah are a blessing and encouragers to me and A Great Love and have been for many years. Eva, because of you, this masterpiece is finished and presented to the nations for such a time as this.

To all God's people of prayer, thank you for your diligence in pursuing the call of Intercession. Without inter-cessors God's work would not manifest itself so freely, as illustrated in this book.

Precept and Practice

Precept and Practice

"And they that shall be of thee shall build the old waste places: thou shalt raise up the foundations of many generations; and thou shalt be called, The repairer of the breach, The restorer of paths to dwell in" (Isaiah 58:12).

One of the many things I love about the Word of God is the plumb line it gives us for our lives. A plumb line is a tool used in the construction trades to determine precise vertical measurement so that the angles of subsequent construction are accurate. Like a plumb line, the Word of God gives us a precise guide in righteous living so that our thoughts, philosophies, and patterns of lifestyle are in line with godliness.

Our God is a God of truth, a lover of truth. Therefore, when we live by the pure Word of truth, we fulfill the divine destinies for our lives and affect the lives of others for His glory. We become builders of His kingdom in new construction as we support and encourage new believers. We also become instrumental in repairing damage caused by the sorrows and challenges that occur in the lives of fellow believers as they build their lives in Christ, ***"...The repairer of the breach, The restorer of paths to dwell in."***

As a disciple of Jesus Christ, one who is a born again believer, you have made a commitment in your heart to follow Him and to become like Him. You find that you are called to intercede for others and God begins to bless your intercession. As intercessors, we become instruments in the hands of Almighty God, standing in the gap between man and his destruction until restoration is completed.

What is intercession? In order to gain any real understanding about intercession, we need to first define it. The following are definitions of intercession as used in biblical text.

> The Hebrew word ***paga*** means *to make intercession, to entreat, to meet together, to come between.* It also means, *to pray, reach, or run,* and *to come up against or to strike against, to be violent against, light or fall upon.*

> The corresponding Greek words ***entunchaneo*** and ***huperentunchaneo*** mean *a meeting between, to meet with, to come between, to meet on behalf of one concerning one, for one, for one's sake, in one's stead.*

> The Greek word ***enteuxis*** means *to get the ear of the king on behalf of another.*

> *Merriam-Webster's Collegiate Dictionary* defines intercession as *prayer, petition, or entreaty in favor of another.*

In considering these definitions, we could summarize intercession as one person standing in place of another in prayer and supplication. When we make supplications in prayer, we state, decree, and request specific needs on our behalf or that of another. They are earnest prayers for particular blessings and benefits, seeking the favor of God. Intercession, in the context of prayer, specifically focuses on supplication unto God for someone else rather than oneself. It is never passive, but rather seeks to do or accomplish something on someone else's behalf.

Dimensions of Intercession

One dimension of intercession concentrates on Hebrews 4:16. That dimension is coming boldly to the presence of Almighty God with our petitions.

"Let us therefore come boldly before the throne of grace, that we may obtain mercy, and find grace to help in the time of need" (Hebrews 4:16).

We have obtained the right and permission to come to Him directly because, as followers of Jesus, we have become sons and daughters of God through the accomplished work of Jesus, His death, burial and resurrection. We bring our petitions before Him directly, without needing an intermediary, and have the confidence of knowing He hears us and keeps His promises.

Another dimension of intercession can be found in the sixth chapter of Ephesians.

"For we wrestle not against flesh and blood, but against principalities, against powers, against the rulers of the darkness of this world, against spiritual wickedness in high places" (Ephesians 6:12).

By the Word of God, the Name of Jesus, and the power of the Holy Spirit, we uphold each other's arms in intercession, and we have victory. As an intercessor, there should be only one outcome indelibly imprinted in your mind. That word is VICTORY! Through the Word of God, the Name of Jesus, and the power of the Holy Spirit, no battle is lost; there is only victory. An example of this is the account of Israel's first battle after leaving Egypt.

"Then came Amalek, and fought with Israel in Rephidim.

And Moses said unto Joshua, Choose out men, and go out, fight with Amalek: tomorrow I will stand on the top of the hill with the rod of God in mine hand.

So Joshua did as Moses had said to him, and fought with Amalek: and Moses, Aaron, and Hur went up to the top of the hill.

And it came to pass, when Moses held up his hand, that Israel prevailed: and when he let down his hand, Amalek prevailed.

But Moses' hands were heavy; and they took a stone, and put it under him, and he sat thereon; and Aaron and Hur stayed up his hands, the one on one side, and the other on the other side; his hands were steady until the going down of the sun.

And Joshua discomfited Amalek and his people with the edge of the sword.

And the Lord said unto Moses, Write this for a memorial in a book, and rehearse it in the ears of Joshua: for I will utterly put out the remembrance of Amalek from under heaven.

And Moses built an altar, and called the name of it Jehovah-nissi:

For he said, Because the Lord hath sworn that the Lord will have war with Amalek from generation to generation" (Exodus 17:8-16).

Moses stood in the authority of God at the top of the hill. As long as he held up his hand, Israel prevailed and they maintained the victory, but his hands became heavy. Clearly it was not a simple short victory and Moses' flesh became weary. Aaron and Hur, in the role of intercessors, provided a stone for Moses to sit and they were committed to holding up his hands for as long as it took the battle to end. Because of their commitment, Moses' hands were steady until sunset, which enabled Joshua and the Israelite army to win the battle. Victory was assured through the steadfast intervention of Aaron and Hur. What an example for us today!

In Hebrew, Amalek means *flesh*. When we become born again, the battle against our flesh begins. There are times when we become weary and need someone to strengthen our hands (our actions and spiritual directives) in the battle. As is declared in Exodus 17, the war with flesh is on-going and the battle for righteousness ends in victory as intercessors do their part. Upon winning the battle, Moses set up a memorial altar and called it Jehovah-nissi, meaning the Lord, Our Banner. The Lord is the standard raised on our behalf and God promises to **"utterly put out the remembrances of Amalek (flesh)" (Exodus 17:14).** As helpers together in earnest prayer and supplication, our victory is sure because our God is our Lord: Jehovah-nissi.

Some interesting meanings of *"utterly put out"* include *to be removed, wiped out, destroyed, put away, and to be smeared with fat.* I shout for joy every time I think of this! The anointing has a major part in destroying the works of the flesh. Through the Spirit we mortify (put to death; make like cement where nothing grows) the deeds of the body (works of flesh). Consider the completeness of such a "wipe out." Every living thing on the surface of Earth was blotted out by the flood (Genesis 7:22, 23). Jesus blotted out the handwriting of ordinances that were against us (Colossians

2:14). When God forgives, He forgets (Isaiah 43:25, 44:22) and it is as if the sin had never occurred.

"And cover not their inquity, and let not their sin be blotted out from before thee: for they have provoked thee to anger before the builders."

"I, even I, am he that blotteth out thy transgressions for mine own sake, and will not remember thy sins."

"I have blotted out, as a thick cloud, thy transgressions, and, as a cloud, thy sins: return unto me; for I have redeemed thee."

This principle is found in First John 1:9 and declares the character of God as compassionate, merciful, and faithful.

"If we confess our sins, he is faithful and just to forgive us our sins, and cleanse us from all unrighteousness" (1 John 1:9).

As we confess our sins, God forgives. Psalm 89:33, 34 confidently assures us that He will never betray His Word or His faithfulness. To be cleansed from all unrighteousness involves being cleansed from every effect that sin has on our lives. It is certainly no wonder that this results in great worship and humility.

"Thou has multiplied the nation, and not increased the joy: they joy before thee according to the joy in harvest, and as men rejoice when they divide the spoil" (Isaiah 9:3).

Victory results in rejoicing and worship. Moses rejoiced in his victory, set up an altar and worshipped the source of his victory, Jehovah-nissi.

Earnest Supplication

A most remarkable example of earnest supplication in intercession is in Acts 12:5 where Peter was imprisoned and prayer was made on his behalf. After Herod had James, the brother of John, put to death, he imprisoned Peter during the Passover season. Peter was bound in chains and under heavy guard. The situation was very grim indeed.

"So Peter was kept in prison: but fervent prayer for him was persistently made to God by the church (assembly)" (Acts 12:5 AMP).

Peter was supernaturally released from his bonds as a result of earnest supplication and the saints who prayed were astonished when Peter showed up at their door.

Such persistent prayer and supplication means that one is stretched out intently. Every fiber of spirit, soul, and body is given with great intensity as with fire. There are no effectual distractions possible during this type of prayer. One is focused, single-minded, and refuses to give up until the answer comes. This manner of prayer releases the angels of God to work for the answer as they did for Peter. Bondage, shackles, and chains fall off. People not only receive an announcement of liberty, but are literally released from the prisons to go forward in the will of God for their lives. The response of those who know them is often astonishment and gladness.

Jesus, the Great Intercessor

Intercession is not a law; it is not an absolute requirement for a believer. It is a glorious privilege that is peculiar to the church dispensation in that power and authority in spiritual realms are now freely available for the New Covenant believers. Before Jesus, intercession was limited to prophets and to the Levitical priesthood, but the ministry of intercession as we know it today began when Jesus Christ ascended to the right hand of the Father, God Almighty.

"Wherefore he is also able to save them to the uttermost that come unto God by him, seeing he ever liveth to make intercession for them" (Hebrews 7:25).

No matter how much Satan attempts to accuse us before God, the Great Intercessor stands between God and Satan on our behalf. While Jesus is interceding in heaven, we should be interceding in the world.

"Herein is our love made perfect, that we may have boldness in the day of judgment: because as he is, so are we in this world" (1 John 4:17).

If we in this world are to be as He is, then intercession must become a priority in our daily lives.

Blessings of Stewardship

Being an intercessor does not need an announcement. In other words, when you decide to give yourself to intercession, you will find that God begins to use and honor you as such. Suddenly people will be moved upon by the Holy Spirit to contact you with prayer requests and burdens. You will not have to announce your calling as intercessor, but rather you will become like a magnet that draws people and their needs to you.

> *"We then that are strong ought to bear the infirmities of the weak, and not to please ourselves" (Romans 15:1).*

> *"Brethren, if any man be overtaken in a fault, ye which are spiritual, restore such an one in the spirit of meekness; considering thyself, lest thou also be tempted" (Galatians 6:1).*

Through intercession, we bear their burdens and we are fulfilling the law of Jesus Christ, that is, the law of love.

When Jesus prayed, people sought after Him. The Holy Spirit in Him became like a magnet drawing people who needed His ministry.

> *"And in the morning, rising up a great while before day, he went out, and departed into a solitary place, and there prayed.*

> *And Simon and they that were with him followed after him.*

> *And when they had found him, they said unto him, All men seek for thee:" (Mark 1:35-37).*

Jesus made prayer His first priority of the day and as a result His ministry prevailed and prospered. It was a regular part of His life, not just an occasional event. Once you have dedicated yourself to spending time alone with God in intercession, you have to maintain it. If you cease from prayer, the Lord will stop using you and channel His blessings through others who are faithful to their prayer life with Him. This kind of honor, the Lord using you, comes from

Him alone. No one can take that honor unto himself or herself; it is only by the Spirit of the Lord.

Man's Cry for an Intercessor

People in the world are looking for people in the Body of Christ who understand the counsel of God and fellowship with Him, particularly when they face the trials, burdens, and temptations of life. The book of Job shows us the condition of mankind searching for someone to fill that gap.

"Neither is there any daysman betwixt us, that might lay his hand upon us both" (Job 9:33).

Job longed for and cried out to God for a "daysman," which means a mediator or an intercessor. He longed for someone who understood God and could bring the two together in counsel. The generations of mankind have not changed. People still search for a "daysman" to stand in the gap and intercede for them, bringing their faces, names, and circumstances before Almighty God.

This brings to mind an occasion of where I was asked to pray for a woman who was very distraught. I didn't even know what kind of counsel to give her. I began to pray and seek the Lord for wisdom. He instructed me to hold her left hand in my right hand and be positioned side by side. Then I prayed in the Spirit and the Lord told me that His life flowed through me into her like a blood transfusion. The Lord also showed me that the idea of real blood transfusions was inspired by Him for the good of mankind. Intercession is life producing and flows from the spirit in you to the person or situation.

No situation is beyond God's power to intervene and bring a transfusion of power into it.

"For in that he himself hath suffered being tempted, he is able to succour them that are tempted" (Hebrews 2:18).

Jesus, who walked on Earth as a man, was "well acquainted" with our weaknesses. He understands our sufferings and temptations because He endured the struggles of humanity and triumphed over them all. That is why He is the Great Intercessor. In intercession, His compassion and understanding flows through us, causing us to rise up and become intercessors.

Judge Not!

Here is a nugget of truth. If you intercede for someone and then become critical or judgmental about that person, you cannot expect to have victory. God will not honor you and you are wasting your time praying for them. I learned this in a specific incident from the Holy Spirit and it was confirmed by the Word of God.

I received a phone call and was asked to intercede for a young man who was born again and baptized in the Holy Spirit as a child. Over time he began to slip away from the Lord through wrong friendships and drugs. Eventually, he began to steal in order to support his drug habit. As a result of the earnest prayers of his parents and loved ones, the Lord appeared to him in prison. He repented and restored his relationship with God and by the supernatural intervention of Almighty God, he was delivered from prison.

He had not been released from prison for long before I received a call to intercede for him because he had fallen back into his old habits. I fell on my knees to pray for him. However, my mind was rambling, *"How could he fall back into his old ways again after You had worked such glorious miracles in his life? You have done so much for him!"* Because of these thoughts, a wall went up and I was unable to step into real intercession for him. The Lord was not allowing it. Suddenly the Lord spoke to me saying, *"Until you stop asking Me, 'Why has he fallen into that?' you cannot, and will not make effective intercession for him."*

"Who art thou that judgest another man's servant? To his own master he standeth or falleth. Yea, he shall be holden up: for God is able to make him stand" (Romans 14:4).

It hit me that I was judging that individual. I felt the tugging, dragging weight of guilt as I entered the throne room of God on behalf of this young man. I was not operating in compassion and godly love for him in his human weakness, and not seeing him through the eyes of Christ. I set myself up as his judge and that is a very dangerous position to take before Almighty God. I immediately repented and the Spirit of earnest intercession fell on me. I then could effectually petition God on his behalf and could effectually war against the powers of darkness for him.

It is wise for intercessors to remember that Deity came and died for **all** humanity. DEITY! Think of it –that puts a very high premium on people in all walks of life. Judging others is a very powerful, albeit negative force, whether we realize it or not. We must remember that Deity came and died for people who, for a variety of reasons, are difficult.

Intercession is a positive force, the life of God flowing from Him through you to that individual. A prime example is in Acts 5, where the sick were being healed by the mere shadow of Peter falling upon them.

"And by the hands of the apostles were many signs and wonders wrought among the people; (and they were all with one accord in Solomon's porch.

And of the rest durst no man join himself to them: but the people magnified them.

And believers were the more added to the Lord, multitudes both of men and women.)

Insomuch that they brought forth the sick into the streets, and laid them on beds and couches, that at the least the shadow of Peter passing by might overshadow some of them.

There came also a multitude out of the cities round about unto Jerusalem, bringing sick folks, and them which were vexed with unclean spirits: and they were healed every one" (Acts 5: 14-16).

I do not believe that it was merely Peter's shadow that did the healing, but rather the force of the glory of God that permeated from him. I remember ministering in Temple, Texas one Sunday morning. After the service, the pastor informed me of a miracle that occurred as I prayed. A woman who was sitting in the front row next to him had a cancerous tumor on her hand. While I passed her and was praying, she said that the growth literally popped off and rolled on to the floor. What a privilege to be used by God in such a magnificent way!

Our Priestly Inheritance

"And from Jesus Christ, who is the faithful witness, and the first begotten of the dead, and the prince of the kings of the earth. Unto him that loved us, and washed us from our sins in his own blood,

And hath made us kings and priests unto God and his Father; to him be glory and dominion for ever and ever. Amen" (Revelation 1:5,6).

It is important for believers to understand the meaning of being kings and priests as declared in Revelation 1:6, since it is what God declares about us. It is easy to understand what a king is, but what is a priest? Kings represent authority, but priests are ones who worship God and intercede on behalf of the people they serve. As kings, we have been given authority through the Name of Jesus (John 14). Besides that, we have been given the right to come boldly to the throne of God and into the presence of His glory.

Under the Old Testament, God had chosen Israel to be a nation that had a priesthood. He made a covenant with Israel whereby the tribe of Levi was separated as a priestly class, given specific rituals of purification from sin for individuals and the nation as a whole. These rituals needed to be continuously performed. The High Priest would be allowed to enter the Holy of Holies behind the great veil once a year and sprinkle the blood of sacrifice for the atonement of sin for the nation.

The veil that separated mankind from God in the Temple of Jerusalem was torn in two at the death of Jesus. Access to God through the Levitical priesthood was finished and we have open and free entry.

"And the veil of the temple was rent in twain from the top to the bottom" (Mark 15:38).

Because Jesus gave the ultimate sacrifice of Himself for all time, there is no longer the need for a priesthood to ritually make sacrifices for the remission of sins. In Jesus, we have been given the priestly inheritance of praying for others. We have direct access to the throne of God, not only to come into His presence, but to come before His throne of grace, obtaining favor, mercy and help in time of need.

"Let us therefore come boldly unto the throne of grace, that we may obtain mercy, and find grace to help in time of need" (Hebrews 4:16).

The word *boldly* in Greek (*tharrheo*) means *to be of good cheer, to be of good courage.* In other words, *to be successful,* so that when we come boldly as priests unto God, we come successfully, cheerfully and with courage.

Just how much has been accomplished in the kingdom of God through intercessory prayer can only be realized when we get to heaven. I wonder, though, how much has gone unaccomplished because many in the Body of Christ have not taken up the mantle of intercession and stood in the gap for others. Scary thought, isn't it?

The Endless Power of Prayer

Our mindset should reflect our dependent humility towards God in prayer. E. M. Bounds (1835-1913), a great minister who wrote extensively on prayer, stated so beautifully, *"The pride of learning is against the dependant humility of prayer."* As an accomplished attorney, he understood the acquisition of knowledge and the temptation to be prideful in that. Yet as a Methodist minister, he also understood that humility in prayer far supersedes pride in ourselves and natural knowledge we can accumulate. Much of the will of God being accomplished in the earth with authority and power is dependent on prayer. John Wesley (1703-1791), a prominent founder of the Methodist Movement, said, *"God cannot do anything on this earth without prayer."* Do not ever underestimate yourself as an intercessor. God has need of you!

Prayer Essentials for Prayer Strategies

A strategy is a plan, an approach, or a line of attack for doing something. The book of Jude gives essentials for prayer strategies.

> *"But ye, beloved, building up yourselves on your most holy faith, praying in the Holy Ghost,*
>
> *Keep yourselves in the love of God, looking for the mercy of our Lord Jesus Christ unto eternal life.*
>
> *And of some have compassion, making a difference:*
>
> *And others save with fear, pulling them out of the fire; hating even the garment spotted by the flesh" (Jude 20-23).*

First – Pray in the Holy Spirit. First John 5:14,15 tells us that when we pray according to the Father's perfect will, we know that we already have the answer. He hears us when we pray according to His perfect will.

"And this is the confidence that we have in him, that, if we ask any thing according to his will, he heareth us:

And if we know that he hear us, whatsoever we ask, we know that we have the petitions that we desired of him" (1 John 5:14,15).

When we pray in the Holy Spirit, we cannot help but pray the perfect will of the Father. I begin my prayer in my known language (English), naming the person and the need for which I am praying. I often say, *"I don't know what to pray for as I ought, but I yield myself to you, Holy Spirit, that my spirit may pray by your Spirit."* I then spend time in intercession, praying in other tongues and as He gives me words in English, I pray in English. As I do so, it is the Holy Spirit praying through me in other tongues, and then giving the interpretation in my known language to decree it, or to supplicate my petitions. This is in cooperation with the Holy Spirit and therefore, it must be successful.

Second – We need to keep ourselves in the love of God. Keep, watch, and guard are synonymous. This implies active and continuous monitoring of ourselves so that our hearts remain one with the love of God.

Being unable to express the love of God is bondage and oppression. In 1969, God set me free with the baptism in the Holy Spirit. A wonderful transformation and liberation took place in my life and people would say to me, *"Oh, you'll be cooled off in about six months."* I would say to myself, *"God forbid that I should ever get cooled off the way I was before!"* Liberty, freedom, and emancipation from all bondage includes being able to express your love to God in praise and worship, as well as walking in love towards other people.

How you choose to worship and praise the Lord is between you and Him. Some prefer to be quiet in the presence of the Lord during a worship service, but in deference to others, do not condemn those who dance, clap their hands, or lift their hands in praise before the Lord, assuming that all is done with decency and divine order. We are all precious to the Father, just the way we are. Be yourself and let your brothers and sisters in the Lord have the same liberty as well. The law of love must prevail.

Third – Have compassion and mercy on others. Intercessory prayer is an honor, but holds tremendous responsibility as well. It should not be treated lightly and its core motivation is the compassion of Almighty God.

> *"And others save with fear, pulling them out of the fire; hating even the garment spotted by the flesh" (Jude 23).*

Years ago I had an experience where I had been drawn to intercede for a man in our community. He and his wife attended my Sunday school class, and they had some serious difficulties. His commitment to Christian growth was very inconsistent and so he had difficulties at home as well as in church. His wife had reached a point of desperation. We were interceding that he would be restored to Christ, go back to church, receive the Word of God being taught, and receive the ministry of the Holy Spirit. His wife called me saying, *"My husband has made an appointment to talk with the minister. Please pray for him that he will make a final decision and commitment for God."*

I went to my place of prayer, and while my hand was still on the doorknob, a tremendous burden of intercession fell on me. I fell to my knees before the Lord. As I entered into a strong, fervent intercession, I had a vision. I saw this man's feet and legs dangling over the fires of hell with the flames climbing higher and higher. It was as if the flames had enormous suction power, intensely drawing him into the flames.

Though this was a new experience for me, I knew without a doubt that I must maintain this fervency in prayer until the burden of intercession lifted and God's intention was complete. If not, this man would be pulled right into the fires of eternal damnation. The flames in the vision had already pulled him into the abyss up to his knees.

As I interceded on his behalf, I heard a voice say, *"This is his last chance!"* I knew then that I had to continue holding on to this man in prayer. I travailed in my spirit for quite a long time, but then the moment came when the peace of God's release began to rush over me and flood my soul. The Lord said, *"It is finished."* I had the assurance that this man would not go to hell. The time was 11:10 p.m., one hour after I had entered into strong intercession, and I learned the next day that he recommitted his life to Christ at the exact time the release had come to me in my prayer closet. Hallelujah!

Some time later the Lord instructed me to relate to him what I had seen during my time of intercession for him. As I told him the story, his face became ashen. He realized the great extent the Lord went to that night, just to give him the opportunity to escape eternal damnation and obtain the security of eternal salvation. After our discussion, he made a decision to deepen his commitment to Christ and accept God's perfect will for his life. He and his wife eventually moved from the community, and to my knowledge, they are still serving the kingdom of God. Glory!

It was a blessed joy to be used by the Holy Spirit. This was an example of prophetic intercession, where the Holy Spirit reveals realities to the intercessor by supernatural revelation. I was used by the Holy Spirit in prayer, and as I completely yielded to Him, He opened the realm of the spirit, enabling me to see, hear, and pray God's perfect will by the Holy Spirit.

Offense and Defense

Through early experiences in praying for this brother, I learned the difference between taking the offensive or defensive position. Every time this man would lose ground in his circumstances, we would earnestly pray for him, and then when he would overcome the circumstance, we would stop praying. I learned that when we pray only as the need arises, you are in a defensive posture, reacting to the need. It is taking care of the situation, but not necessarily moving forward.

God definitely let me know that He wants us to move into the offensive position and be proactive in advancing the purposes of the kingdom. In other words, don't always wait for the attack, but rather forcefully advance through intercessory prayer. I once heard someone say, *"He who runs with the football gets tackled."* I chuckled and thought, *"Yes, but he who runs with the football scores the touchdown!"* Praise be unto God!

Controlling the Atmosphere

I do not believe that anyone wants to walk in darkness and disobedience once they have the light of God and His Word in their hearts and lives, and they understand the consequences of poor choices. If someone does walk in darkness and disobedience, they are deceived. However, as we intercede, glorious beams of light are shed forth into darkness. This is how we can control the atmosphere around us. Demonic forces that affect the mood, attitude and decision making of individuals are pushed back as we pray.

Let's be clear about this – we do not have authority over the will of others. Trying to do so is witchcraft. We do, however, have authority over the influencing forces of darkness that affect the ultimate will and way of sinners. As we intercede for them, they are released from the blinding darkness of the demonic influence and become free to make their own choices.

> *"In whom the god of this world hath blinded the minds of them which believe not, lest the light of the glorious gospel of Christ, who is the image of God, should shine unto them" (2 Corinthians 4:4).*

Living in Love and Forgiveness

Intercession is one of the greatest forces leading to love. The more we pray for someone, the more *"...the love of God is shed abroad in our hearts by the Holy Ghost which is given unto us" (Romans 5:5)* for that individual.

You cannot allow bitterness, hurt, resentment, and unforgiveness to reside in your heart, and expect to successfully pray for someone else. If you believe in the power that is in the Word of God and in your prayers, you cannot continue to harbor such negative things inside and expect God's blessings on your prayers. With our eyes firmly fixed on Jesus as our example, we must continually walk in love and forgiveness.

Intercession moves us into the fruit of the Spirit and out of the works of the flesh. It presses us into the nature and image of Jesus Christ. It moves us into the same love that sent Him and kept Him while he was on earth. The love that is in Him is His ability within us to destroy any self-centeredness. It is that love that masters Satan and flesh, moving you into the nature of Jesus.

Prophetic Intercession

There are two dimensions of prophecy, and both lead to edification and the comfort of the receiver of the prophetic utterance. One is telling forth the will of God, the other is fore-telling the will of God. He often reveals what is, but there are also times in prayer when the Lord will lead you to intercede for future events. Prophetic intercession can cause doors of ministry as well as other doors of opportunity to be opened to you. Whether or not we live out our destiny in God is heavily dependent upon our prayer lives. When your prayer life is strong, you are more apt to hear with clarity and then follow the leading of your heart as you are led by the Holy Spirit.

I have had many examples of this in my life, but one particular event comes to mind. In 1974, as I was praying in the Spirit, I had a vision. I saw African style huts and a tall, thin, African man in a running position. It was obvious to me that this vision had something to do with Africa, but that was all that came to me. This vision and intercession continued that year and into the next year.

While in Israel in 1977, I attended a Full Gospel Businessmen's Convention, and there were two Nigerian brothers also in attendance. They were touring with us, and one of them was touring with our group. On the tour, we visited the Upper Room in Jerusalem, and as we formed a circle, the glory and power of God began to fall.

Peter, one of the Nigerians, happened to be standing to my right and a Baptist woman stood to my left. The woman said, *"I don't think I'm saved. Would you please pray for me?"* I just knew that she was indeed saved, but what she really needed was the infilling of the Holy Spirit as a seal of assurance. I told her this and asked her if she wanted to receive the baptism of the Holy Spirit. She agreed and was baptized in the Holy Spirit. No one will now ever convince her that she isn't saved.

At that moment, our leader, a pastor from Oklahoma, motioned for me to come in his direction to pray for another woman to receive the Holy Spirit. He, too, was praying with others. As I prayed for this woman, she gloriously received the baptism in the Holy Spirit. There was a tremendous breakthrough of weeping and rejoicing as the glory of God filled that room.

Suddenly, the Lord spoke to me saying that Peter wanted to be filled with the Holy Spirit. I said, *"Lord, you know Peter is baptized with the Holy Spirit. He is a Full Gospel Businessmen's representative from Nigeria, and all Full Gospel Businessmen are baptized in the Holy Spirit."* The Lord simply repeated what He told me. Thinking that the Lord surely knows something that I didn't, I looked across the room at Peter. As usual, his head was lowered respectfully in response to what was going on in the room, but he didn't really look happy. I then went to Peter, looked into his face and said, *"Peter, the Lord says you want to be baptized in the Holy Spirit. Is this true?"* Of course, it was true, but in my immaturity I had to ask. God's patience with us is infinite.

"Yes," responded Peter. When I heard that, my heart leaped with joy. I stood on my toes, put my finger on his forehead and prayed. His eyes began to well up with tears as he stretched his hands toward heaven. He began to lift his voice

in the heavenly language of the Holy Spirit, praising God. It was a glorious moment!

Two weeks after returning home, I was in prayer and the Lord reminded me of the man in Africa I had been praying for during 1974 and 1975. He said to me, *"Peter was the man that you saw in the Spirit during prayer. I ordered his steps from Benin City, Nigeria, and your steps from Tulsa, Oklahoma. Your paths crossed in Israel, and your prayers and his were consummated when you led him to the baptism in the Holy Spirit."*

Can you imagine my rejoicing when the Lord revealed this to me?

What an unlimited adventure we have as we pray in the Spirit! These are adventures beyond the veil of flesh into the glorious and exciting realm of the unknown. I can emphatically say that in Jesus, the best is yet to come!

Intercession Opens Doors

In January, 1980, I ministered at the International Convention of Faith Ministers and Churches in Florida. A young Nigerian man received my tapes at this conference, and later that year wrote me a letter requesting me to come to Nigeria. He wanted me to teach on the ministry of intercession during the day, and in open-air crusades in the evening. My mind panicked since I knew nothing about open-air crusades. All I was able to envision was the type of crusades held by T. L. Osborne where hundreds of thousands of people gathered together for ministry. I told my administrative assistant to hold that letter of invitation until I could "pray through" about it.

A while later, I remembered a conversation I had with a pastor a few months before. He shared victorious testimonies of God's mighty working power in a crusade in Kenya where he ministered.

Upon remembering this conversation, I thought, *"Could this be the direction of God?"* As I continued in prayer, I believed in my heart that this was a new door of opportunity that God wanted me to walk through.

I wrote to this pastor and he believed that God would have him go to Nigeria with me, and then go on to Kenya for further ministry. Our teams joined in New York in May, 1981, and after an arduous journey, we arrived in Nigeria. It would take volumes to share all of the awesome miracles of God performed on this trip. A most memorable one was when I led a Nigerian king, who had 250 chieftains under his authority, to be born again and filled with the baptism in the Holy Spirit. I had read First Timothy 2:1-5 to him and he requested that I pray with him. Another amazing display of God's power was when a little three year old girl, whose legs were like frozen matchsticks under her buttocks, received a creative miracle and walked for the first time in her life.

Great and Effectual Doors

Prophetic intercessory prayer opens great and effectual doors, but they may also be accompanied by great adversaries. As we were departing from Nigeria, my friend and fellow intercessor discovered that she did not have her "yellow slip of paper" (departure permit). Without it, we were threatened with imprisonment. We were taken to the back of the airport to be roughly interrogated. Fear began to grip my mind. I thought, "Lord, if you don't intervene and give us a miracle, we are going to prison, and I am not called to the prison ministry, especially in Nigeria." I was desperate.

As I was answering the interrogator's questions, I was mentally talking to the Lord. Suddenly, I heard the Lord's voice above the official's rough and insulting voice. The Lord asked me, *"What do you have in your purse?"* The envelope with the king's name, address, and seal upon it flashed into my mind. Fear was swallowed up in perfect love—Almighty God, Himself! I reached into my purse and took out the envelope. I knew that airport official was about to discover that the authority had shifted and it was not in his favor. Through the hand of God, I was now in authority.

I threw the envelope down before the official's eyes. Consternation crept over his face as his eyes became larger. He asked, *"Where did you get this?"*

I responded with higher authority, *"It says right there. The king of Orgefe gave it to me."*

He and I both knew that evil had bowed its knee. He angrily said, *"Go!"* You can believe we did not hesitate or delay. Once again, we knew that God can turn any situation around. Glory be to God!

These experiences began in prophetic intercession in 1974, and were fulfilled in May, 1981, to show me how prophetic intercession not only opens great and effectual doors of ministry, but also deliverance and a way of escape when needed, even when the situation seems very uncertain.

Groaning and Travail in the Spirit—Not the Flesh!

I am asked frequently about experiences intercessors have during their prayer time. *"Why is it that when I am in intercession, I experience many different reactions? Sometimes it's weeping, a broken spirit, a sense of being upset, or whatever. Yet, at other times, there is no reaction at all."* The answer can be found in Galatians.

"My little children, of whom I travail in birth again until Christ be formed in you" *(Galatians 4:19).*

In this passage, the Greek word for travail is *odino,* and it means *to be in pain as in childbirth.*

The Holy Spirit is a person. He can be grieved, He hurts, and He feels, and as you move into the Holy Spirit through intercession, you will experience some of His grief and sorrow for humanity. These experiences can be called travail.

It is important to note that we do not travail in the flesh in prayer, but rather in the Spirit. This process moves from the Spirit, to the mind, to sometimes feeling things physically. It is not something you should try to conjure up. However, if it happens, rejoice knowing that the Holy Spirit is moving you into that burden and will bring release because in intercessory prayer, we are joined together with the Holy Spirit.

I have ministered in places where people worked themselves up in the flesh and it was very obvious. When I ministered to them by the laying on of hands, they would fall into horrible fits supposedly "travailing." I would have to take authority over the spirit that was operating against them. When it is not the Holy Spirit, it is a work of flesh and can appear repulsive. The Holy Spirit's working is never repulsive, is always decent and in order, and always brings a positive end.

The Intercessor and the Worshipper

As intercessors, we need to understand the relationship between prayer and worship. They are not the same. Nevertheless, worship is very significant in the life of an intercessor. When you praise and worship God, you are standing in the ministry of a worshipper, not an intercessor. You are preparing the way for prayer to go forth in victory, producing positive results. Worship causes your whole being to focus on the greatness and wonder of Almighty God. It prepares your heart to be in communion with Him because you are acknowledging His omnipresence, omniscience, and omnipotence. In other words, He is all present, all knowing, and all powerful.

Worship and intercession unite the body of believers like nothing else. It fuses people together in the spirit. Praise and worship frequently arises during intercessory prayer gatherings and sets the atmosphere to accurately hear from heaven. The intercessory prayer group is then able to flow with heavenly directive as one body.

Praise, Worship, and Intercession

"And they rose early in the morning, and went forth into the wilderness of Tekoa: and as they went forth, Jehoshaphat stood and said, Hear me, O Judah, and ye inhabitants of Jerusalem; Believe in the LORD your God, so shall ye be established; believe his prophets, so shall ye prosper.

And when he had consulted with the people, he appointed singers unto the LORD, and that should praise the beauty of holiness, as they went out before the army, and to say, Praise the LORD; for his mercy endureth for ever.

And when they began to sing and to praise, the LORD set ambushments against the children of Ammon, Moab, and mount Seir, which were come against Judah; and they were smitten" (2 Chronicles 20:20-22).

What happens during praise and worship? As we lift up praise, it passes through the principalities, powers, rulers of darkness of this world, and against spiritual wickedness in high places (Ephesians 6:12). It clears a path for our prayers and the blessings of God to flow freely. It opens up the way. Just as the singers went before the Israelite army praising God, which resulted in victory for the army, our praise and worship goes before intercession and we become victorious as well.

Praise also stills the avenger. It causes the enemy to cease, to vanish, to be done away with, and to fail. The praises of Almighty God and the enemy cannot occupy the same atmosphere. The enemy must be silenced in the presence of praise and worship.

"Out of the mouth of babes and sucklings hast thou ordained strength because of thine enemies, that thou mightest still the enemy and the avenger" (Psalm 8:2).

"And said unto him, Hearest thou what these say? And Jesus saith unto them, Yea; have ye never read, Out of the mouth of babes and sucklings thou hast perfected praise?" (Matthew 21:16).

Strength and praise are used in the same position in these two passages. There is strength in praise that silences the forces of darkness.

When we move into worship, our words are pure and then we can also speak the pure words of God. Often during praise gatherings, there are messages in tongues with interpretation. Such gifts are activated because everyone has been brought into unity in the presence of God. His life is imparted and expressed.

When believers press into worship, they are pressing into God's life. We press into healing, preservation, deliverance, soundness, and everything He is. The Lord is our salvation, and that salvation is not only for your eternal soul, but for every area of your life.

We are made whole in our bodies because the Word and resurrection life proceeds from the spirit man. That life begins to work its way out to soul and body. Paul's prayer is our sure anchor of faith for this.

> *"And the very God of peace sanctify you wholly; and I pray God your whole spirit and soul and body be preserved blameless unto the coming of our Lord Jesus Christ.*
>
> *Faithful is he that calleth you, who also will do it" (1 Thessalonians 5:23,24).*

Worship is the Great Temple Sweeper

One of the definitions of worship in Greek is *temple sweeper*. When we worship, it is like the wind of the Spirit of God blowing mightily throughout your temple (your body), sweeping it clean from the debris that clogs an unrenewed mind.

"And be not conformed to this world: but be ye transformed by the renewing of your mind, that ye may prove what is that good, and acceptable, and perfect, will of God" *(Romans 12:2).*

There is no way that we believers can live in this life free from offenses. They come to everybody. When they do, they leave behind all sorts of rubbish or residue. Hurt feelings, unforgiveness, bitterness, and the like, crop up like weeds in our souls, which affect our walk with Christ. As long as we live in this natural world, we will deal with these shortcomings. This is why we need the supernatural manifestation of the Holy Spirit through worship, which enables us to be cleansed from soulish debris. Worship is one of God's powerful cleansing agents, and as we worship, our temples are swept clean.

"Not by works of righteousness which we have done, but according to his mercy he saved us, by the washing of regeneration, and renewing of the Holy Ghost;

Which he shed on us abundantly through Jesus Christ our Saviour;

That being justified by his grace, we should be made heirs according to the hope of eternal life.

This is a faithful saying, and these things I will that thou affirm constantly, that they which have believed in God might be careful to maintain good works. These things are good and profitable unto men" *(Titus 3:5-8).*

As we yield ourselves to be continuously cleansed by His Spirit, it becomes second nature to simply walk in the Spirit.

Ushered Into His Presence

When I was in Israel in 1976, I was given a special invitation through an unusual set of circumstances. I was one out of 365 people invited to attend a prayer meeting in a Catholic church on Mount Zion. People from many nations gathered together to praise, worship, and hear from God.

The room was not very large, but it was wonderfully crafted with a marble floor and bright stained glass windows. As I entered this beautiful church, I stood among people of diverse nationalities and ethnicities including Hasidic Jews. The power of the Lord came upon me, and I went down onto that marble floor. As I lay on the floor, everyone above me was praising and worshipping God in the Spirit. I felt as if I were being lifted up and elevated to the ceiling. I was absolutely surrounded by the presence of God. The Lord said to me, "*You have been elevated into My presence on the sacrifice of the praise and worship of My people.*" After I heard this, it was some time later before I was finally able to stand to my feet. When I did get up, I found myself dancing before the Lord in joyful praise and worship with all of the people.

Praise and worship elevates you into the presence of Almighty God. Spiritual warriors can then go to battle against the forces of darkness with the presence of the Lord going before them. Just as the warriors of Israel would send the worshipping tribe of Judah ahead of them into battle. The battle was fought and the victory was won.

"And His brightness was like the sunlight; rays streamed from His hand, and there [in the sunlike splendor] was the hiding place of His power" (Habakkuk 3:4 AMP).

That is intercession. It is an extension of the mighty right hand of God. We build ourselves up in our prayer closets, interceding for one another. Then we go forth in the power of the Great Arm and Hand extended to the world and among believers. It is intercession in action.

Jesus is the Cornerstone

In intercession we obtain the power of God to be, do, think, and act like Jesus. I once asked the Lord, *"Father, with all the doctrinal error and confusion that is going on in the Body today, how can your people stay free from all this, recognizing false doctrine apart from the doctrine of Christ?"*

He answered, *"If it is of Me, it will look like Me. They will be doing the works that I have done, and they will walk in the authority and anointing that I walk in."*

Having been a believer and minister sent to many parts of the world for quite some time, I have seen many things, some not of God. The devil can conjure up a lot of lying signs and wonders, but he can never counterfeit the anointing. A fellow once said, *"I may not know when it is, but I definitely know when it ain't!"*

We determine scriptural truth by measuring it up to Jesus. It is the way you can really know. Jesus is the cornerstone by which we should measure all things. Cornerstones establish a true right angle and the sides of the building have to line up with it so that they are straight. So it is with

Jesus being the cornerstone. All doctrines must line up with Him to be straight.

> *"Wherefore also it is contained in the scripture, Behold, I lay in Sion a chief corner stone, elect, precious: and he that believeth on him shall not be confounded"* *(1 Peter 2:6).*

It is vital, therefore, to know Him intimately. Know His Word and spend time communicating with Him in His presence. He is the Great Intercessor and, therefore, is the Great Communicator. Jesus is all of what is declared in Isaiah 9:6 (Wonderful, Counselor, mighty God, everlasting Father, Prince of Peace), but all of these attributes represent intercession in action. It is summarized in Paul's writing to the Hebrews.

> *"Wherefore he is able also to save them to the uttermost that come unto God by him, seeing he ever liveth to make intercession for them" (Hebrews 7:25).*

The works that Jesus did, we are to do because *"as He is, so are we in this world"* (1 John 4:17). Furthermore, Jesus said the following of believers:

> *"Verily, verily, I say unto you, He that believeth on me, the works that I do shall he do also; and greater works than these shall he do; because I go unto my Father"* *(John 14:12).*

Jesus is speaking to us and about us. We are to do the works of Jesus on the earth, but the foundation for everything we set our hands to accomplish in this life is laid in intercession. A believer, a church, a minister, or a ministry will never rise above or beyond their level of intercessory prayer and the knowledge of His Word. That is the plumb line.

Grow in Faith

Where do you begin? You begin by walking by faith. We must locate ourselves first, realizing where we are in our faith walk. To over estimate our faith status is dangerous because hope can become deferred when we don't really have the faith to receive what we have asked for. Then we don't receive anything. Not only is that disappointing, but gives the enemy opportunity to creep into our thoughts, lying to us about how this "faith stuff" doesn't work. Underestimating is just as bad because it prevents you from launching forward. It makes you timid and defeated before you even begin.

Wherever you are in your walk, faith increases as we continue in His Word, meditate on it, put it into our spirits, and act on it. We start out believing God for the small things, and continue to grow and mature to a place where we are able to believe Him for greater things.

> *"Looking unto Jesus the author and finisher of our faith; who for the joy that was set before him endured the cross, despising the shame, and is set down at the right hand of the throne of God"* *(Hebrews 12:2).*

Jesus wants us to look to Him. As we do, we become close to Him. Our confidence of this is secured by James 4:8, where it says, *"Draw nigh to God, and he will draw nigh to you*...." His anointing that already abides within, according to First John 2:27, begins to rise to the forefront. We then begin to take on His expressed image in the earth, so that the Light of the world can shine bright within us. It begins with intercession as we draw close to Him in prayer.

Accountability

General Douglas MacArthur, one of the great generals of WWII, said, *"The history of failure in war can be summed up in two words, TOO LATE; too late in comprehending the deadly purposes of a potential enemy; too late in realizing the mortal danger; too late in preparedness; too late in uniting all possible forces for resistance; too late in standing with one's friends."* How true this is in prayer as well. The principle that General MacArthur's statement makes is about responsibility and accountability of each individual.

We are accountable for the knowledge we acquire, for the gifts we have been given, and for the callings we have received.

> *"For the invisible things of him from the creation of the world are clearly seen, being understood by the things that are made, even his eternal power and Godhead; so that they are without excuse:" (Romans 1:20).*

The Holy Spirit is crying out to the Body of Christ, wooing and drawing each member unto Himself to be intercessors. His desire and call is to quicken and enable us to be a people who are not "too late" in comprehending the deadly purposes of a potential enemy, the powers of darkness; not "too late" in preparedness of the Word of God, the Sword of the Spirit; not "too late" in uniting all possible forces for resistance; and not "too late" in standing with one's friends, united in the power of the Holy Spirit. Therefore, we need to be "***...strong in the Lord, and in the power of His might,***" (Ephesians 6:10), interceding for one another as the Holy Spirit continuously leads us to do so. We will then prevent and avoid many pitfalls and defeats planned by the evil strategist, Satan, against the church of the living God, and we will build the kingdom of our God.

Jonathan G. Edwards (1703-1758), distinguished revivalist during the Great Awakening of the 18th century, said, "*When God has something very great to accomplish for His church, it is His will that there should precede it, the extraordinary prayers of His people. And it is revealed that when God is about to accomplish great things for His church, He will begin by remarkably pouring out the Spirit of grace and supplication.*"

> "***And I will pour upon the house of David, and upon the inhabitants of Jerusalem, the spirit of grace and of supplications: and they shall look upon me whom they have pierced, and they shall mourn for him, as one mourneth for his only son, and shall be in bitterness for him, as one that is in bitterness for his firstborn***" (***Zechariah 12:10***).

The Spirit was poured on both the house of David (Jews) and the inhabitants of Jerusalem (Gentiles). It is a Spirit available to all believers in Him who died for us. When we made that decision to be a follower of Jesus, that same Spirit of grace and supplication was poured into our spirits. The Great Intercessors, Jesus and the Holy Spirit, live in us to intercede. When Lazarus was raised from the dead, someone had to "***loose him and let him go***" (John 11:44). In a similar manner, we have to loose the Great Intercessors from within us and let them go and together we accomplish great and mighty things.

John Wesley (1703-1791), one of the founders of the
Methodist Movement, preached that God is dependent upon
our prayers, and can't do anything in this earth unless man
asks Him to do it. By our will we can tie the hands of God
and keep blessings from coming to us. Each of us has a free
will, and we can choose to yield to the prompting of the Holy
Spirit or not. We have control over our own will and can
choose to obey the will of God in prayer.

Birthing Prophecy

In the 1970's, God began to speak to me about the
power of prayer as related to birthing prophecies. As He
unfolded this revelation to me, I began to comprehend the
principal in His Word that prophecy is conditional. One
condition for its fulfillment is that it must be birthed in
prayer.

Today, as I look back over the years where God has
used me to prophesy over people, places, and nations, I think
of Sweden. I have been there many times over the years and
because they respect the call upon my life, they expect God
to use me to prophesy each time I go to minister. These
people are mightily used of God in Scandinavia and many
other nations.

God uses me there to confirm what He has already
spoken and revealed to the people of God. I observed that
each prophecy and confirmation I had given to the pastor
and his people came to pass. When I asked the Lord about
that He said, "They come to pass because they believe it,
they receive it, they pray, and they act like it is so." Therein,
are the ingredients for fulfilled prophecy.

Once when I ministered there in Sweden I had a
vision where I saw a train crossing the sanctuary. I shared

the vision with the congregation and prophesied concerning it. I was later told that they had previously received instructions from the Lord to take a train to Siberia for ministry and my vision confirmed it. However, since this was before the Soviet Union was dismantled there was a serious obstacle. The KGB was in control of the only track to Siberia. Time passed, and one day a man came into the church. He said to the pastor, "I hear you want a train." The pastor acknowledged that he did, the man said that he was from the KGB and could get them the train. When I returned there months later, approximately 100 people left for Siberia with their train and visited twelve cities. Many received Christ and the people in two of the cities had never even heard of the Name of Jesus.

As I pursued the Lord's leading about understanding birthing prophecy through prayer, I asked Him questions about it. He directed me to Daniel 9 for enlightenment.

> *"In the first year of Darius the son of Ahasuerus, of the seed of the Medes, which was made king over the realm of the Chaldeans;*
>
> *In the first year of his reign I Daniel understood by books the number of the years, whereof the word of the LORD came to Jeremiah the prophet, that he would accomplish seventy years in the desolations of Jerusalem.*
>
> *And I set my face unto the Lord God, to seek by prayer and supplications, with fasting, and sackcloth, and ashes:"* *(Daniel 9:1-3).*

God had spoken through the prophet Jeremiah that Israel would go into 70 years of captivity, and afterwards would be delivered. That appears to be unconditional prophecy. God stated specific actions and timing. Later, the prophet Daniel, in searching the "books," understood the times of the Lord and what should be done to secure these prophetic times into manifested reality.

Daniel set his face to the Lord God, and sought Him by prayers and supplications. In seeing this, God showed me that Daniel had birthed Jeremiah's prophecy into reality. I was amazed as He let me know this was a primary condition in prophecy coming to pass. It must be birthed in prayer. I then said, *"Lord, you spoke prophecy in Genesis 3:15 about the coming of our blessed Redeemer. I don't believe anyone birthed that prophecy, but it came to pass just as you said."*

He asked, *"Is that right?"*

I said, *"Yes, sir."*

He then said, *"Why don't you go to Luke Two and read."* As I did so, the Holy Spirit within me exploded understanding and revelation. Luke Two is the story of the presentation of the child Jesus in the temple according to the law. While bringing Jesus into the temple, Mary and Joseph encountered Simeon.

> *"And, behold, there was a man in Jerusalem, whose name was Simeon; and the same man was just and devout, waiting for the consolation of Israel: and the Holy Ghost was upon him.*
>
> *And it was revealed unto him by the Holy Ghost, that he should not see death, before he had seen the Lord's Christ.*

And he came by the Spirit into the temple: and when the parents brought in the child Jesus, to do for him after the custom of the law,

Then took he him up in his arms, and blessed God, and said,

Lord, now lettest thou thy servant depart in peace, according to thy word:

For mine eyes have seen thy salvation,

Which thou hast prepared before the face of all people;

A light to lighten the Gentiles, and the glory of thy people Israel" (Luke 2:25-32).

As I read further, I found that Anna, the prophetess, was also vitally important to the events of that day.

"And there was one Anna, a prophetess, the daughter of Phanuel, of the tribe of Aser: she was of a great age, and had lived with an husband seven years from her virginity;

And she was a widow of about fourscore and four years, which departed not from the temple, but served God with fastings and prayers night and day.

And she coming in that instant gave thanks likewise unto the Lord, and spake of him to all them that looked for redemption in Jerusalem" (Luke 2:36-38).

With great joy, I knew that Simeon and Anna had been used by God to birth the Genesis 3:15 prophecy about the Lord. Others may also have prayed for the Redeemer to come, and no doubt had, but Simeon and Anna are specifically recorded for our understanding. What a tremendous answer to prayer. Not only did God keep His promise to Simeon in allowing him to behold the Messiah, He allowed the child to be laid into Simeon's arms so that he would bless Him before heaven and earth and speak into the life of His mother.

God showed me that he would also raise up a people to birth the great end time event in prayer. In fact, Isaiah 52:8 took on new meaning.

"Thy watchmen shall lift up the voice; with the voice together shall they sing: for they shall see eye to eye, when the LORD shall bring again Zion" (Isaiah 52:8).

Intercessors will be in unity and they shall see together eye to eye, the return of the Lord. Just as Simeon and Anna recognized the Savior as an infant, so today, the praying people of intercession are ones who recognize the move of God when it comes. Glory be to God.

The Holy Spirit, who guides us into all truth, gave me more revelation about the end time prophecy "birthers." He led me to Isaiah 59, Ephesians 6, and First Thessalonians 5. All three passages speak of armor and the character of God that we acquire and use.

"And he saw that there was no man, and wondered that there was no intercessor: therefore his arm brought salvation unto him; and his righteousness, it sustained him.

For he put on righteousness as a breast-plate, and an helmet of salvation upon his head; and he put on the garments of vengeance for clothing, and was clad with zeal as a cloak" (Isaiah 59:16,17).

"Finally, my brethren, be strong in the Lord, and in the power of his might.

Put on the whole armour of God, that ye may be able to stand against the wiles of the devil.

For we wrestle not against flesh and blood, but against principalities, against powers, against the rulers of the darkness of this world, against spiritual wickedness in high places.

Wherefore take unto you the whole armour of God, that ye may be able to withstand in the evil day, and having done all, to stand.

Stand therefore, having your loins girt about with truth, and having on the breastplate of righteousness;

And your feet shod with the preparation of the gospel of peace;

Above all, taking the shield of faith, wherewith ye shall be able to quench all the fiery darts of the wicked.

And take the helmet of salvation, and the sword of the Spirit, which is the word of God:

Praying always with all prayer and supplication in the Spirit, and watching thereunto with all perseverance and supplication for all saints;" (Ephesians 6:10-18).

In both Isaiah 59 and Ephesians 6, the armor and the battle are not physical, but rather spiritual. Jesus, as Savior, walked in righteousness, fully armored daily against the powers of darkness and is the ultimate intercessor who closed the gap between mankind and God. The believer must put on the same armor that was on Jesus. This is done by having a prayer life. It is accomplished as we walk in truth, righteousness, faith, peace, and obedience.

First Thessalonians repeats the same sentiment, but adds that we are of the day, meaning that we have a specific destiny in end times. It also gives the directive that while it is still day (before the end), we must be sober. This means that we must be vigilant, aware, serious about God's Word, and have self-restraint and self-control to accomplish our purpose.

"Ye are all the children of light, and the children of the day: we are not of the night, nor of darkness.

Therefore let us not sleep, as do others; but let us watch and be sober.

For they that sleep sleep in the night; and they that be drunken are drunken in the night.

But let us, who are of the day, be sober, putting on the breastplate of faith and love; and for an helmet, the hope of salvation" (1 Thessalonians 5:5-8).

We are "of the day" spiritually fighting the powers of darkness, who are "of the night." We have a vital role to play in the second coming of Jesus because we are birthing and ushering in the glory of the Lord that precedes the rapture of the church. As we intercede for laborers to come into the harvest (Luke 10:2), for the anointing and scriptural prophecies to be fulfilled in the lives of God's people, we prepare the coming of the Lord.

Personal Prophecies

Praying prophecies into reality is also for individuals. Prophecies are like precious pearls from heaven spoken over you, your loved ones, or your church. They are the plans and purposes God has for your life. God declares these particular things over you when a prophecy goes forth. However, unless you birth that prophecy through intercessory prayer, speaking the Word of God, standing in faith for it, and waging a good warfare by it, you will never see it come to pass.

So many people have received beautiful, grand and glorious prophecies of the Lord, but because they didn't know that they had a part in its fulfillment, they simply waited without exercising faith to receive from God. When we pray, intercede, and obey the leading of the Lord, faith rises and the fulfillment of the promise can come to pass.

To fight, to wrestle, to beat against something, to contend with the adversary—these are all attributes of the warrior side of intercession. When we intercede, we come against the forces of darkness, those demonic powers, that have an individual or a situation bound up against the will of Almighty God. Intercession clears the path for God's blessings and faith brings them in.

"Let us therefore come boldly unto the throne of grace, that we may obtain mercy, and find grace to help in time of need" (Hebrews 4:16).

Having the opportunity to come boldly to the throne of God is the positive dimension of intercession. Why come boldly to God's throne? To receive grace. But what is grace? Grace is God's giving love gifts to us. It is His divine favor, His peace, and His prosperity in every area, spirit, soul, and body. God's grace is His help, ability, strength, and sufficiency. God's grace is everything we are not and do not naturally possess. We are to come boldly to the throne of grace for ourselves and on behalf of others, so that we may receive gifts of love from the Father. When we come away from the throne, we can rest assured that we have released "love gifts" from heaven.

As we intercede for others, we are birthing things into their lives to help them reach their full potential in God. This does not necessarily mean that there is something wrong with that person. Without intercession, a believer's full potential of spiritual growth is limited. They reach a plateau and go no further without the added dimension intercession brings. This is not only true for individuals, but has the same effect on church growth and maturity as well. Many times ministries fail because there is no one interceding for the minister, their ministry of helps, and the ministry itself, even though they are truly called and ordained by God. Again, a minister, a saint of God, a church, or a ministry will never rise above or beyond their level of intercessory prayer. As we pray and stay pure before God, He can and will do great and mighty things.

I am sometimes amused and also often saddened by some people's ideas of intercession. For many years, some thought the ministry of intercession was for those people in the church who were either too old or too sick to do anything else. So their designated job in church was to simply stay home and "remember people in prayer." Now there is nothing wrong with the elderly at home spending time in prayer for others. In fact, some of those elderly saints are powerhouses and you would want their prayers. However, when it is the sole designation for intercessors, there is a problem. Intercession is for everyone.

Another thought was that intercessors were women who had nothing better to do than mind somebody else's business. They imagined such women coming together over coffee and crumpets to discuss the problems of brother so-and-so or sister what's-her-name, all under the banner of "we need to remember them in prayer." They then all bow their heads for a moment to recite a prayer over the newly roasted victims of glorified gossip, and go merrily on their way. To be sure, this abuse has occurred in places, but this is not intercession. Not by a long shot! Neither is the ministry of intercession for those who do not qualify for another position.

Intercession is work, co-laboring with God to bring about a victorious result in the life of another. That work reaches, touches, and changes the lives of countless people. Countless means just that – too many to count. Intercession is so important that it is a ministry for every single believer who ever was or is to come.

> *"And hope maketh not ashamed; because the love of God is shed abroad in our hearts by the Holy Ghost which is given unto us" (Romans 5:5).*

As an intercessor, God will cause you to dream big and see big, expecting big results from Him. That is because God speaks and declares *"those things which be not as though they were" (Romans 4:17).* We must be careful to guard ourselves against microscopic vision, that is, to see only in the parameters of our own minds. We must remain focused on the promise and not let go until it is birthed into the natural. God said, *"...My counsel shall stand, and I will do all my pleasure" (Isaiah 46:10).*

So often, when God reveals His ultimate plan for us or for a situation, there is no way in the natural we can ever see it happening. This is where faith must work. When you pray and intercede, you begin to see things from God's perspective, and to think the way He thinks. You begin to act the way He acts and talk the way He talks. The closer you walk with Him, the more you will find yourself enlarging your vision. The way you do this is to continuously feed your spirit with His promises, praying also in the Spirit, so that you can see as He does.

Unity in the Spirit

As we become as one voice through the understanding of the Word, and through the ministry of the Holy Spirit, we grow as one in intercession. We then see great and mighty things take place.

I remember a specific occasion when it was snowing and I was on my way to a prayer meeting. The Lord specifically told me not to pray for anything in the group, but just to praise and worship. When I arrived I informed the others in the group. As we began to sing in the spirit, the sound of the song took on a very specific sound similar to that of Native American song. The Lord let me know that it was a victory war dance song. One of the women contacted a Sioux friend asking about it and she was informed that indeed this sound was like the victory war dance song that Sioux men would sing before they went out to battle.

This came up again at another prayer meeting. I attended Rhema Bible Training Center, and prayer was held every Monday night. As we prayed together for a few weeks, we began to experience unity in the Spirit at our meetings. One evening in particular stands out in my mind.

After much intercession, suddenly everyone in the room became silent. You could have heard a pin drop. This must have lasted about twenty minutes. All of a sudden the silence was broken by a single voice, singing a song in the Spirit. One by one, others joined in the singing. It came across the auditorium like a giant ocean wave. It became one melodious voice in the Spirit.

Some time later, I was visiting a couple who had never been to these Monday night meetings. That evening we began to pray and intercede together. While in intercession, the man began to sing that same melody that had been sung during that monumental night of intercessory prayer at Rhema Bible Training Center. He then sang the interpretation in English, which was, *"This is the victory song; this is the victory dance. Join in and sing the victory song; the victory dance."* That explained what happened in the service at Rhema. We had received the victory through intercession, and then began to sing the victory song, praising, worshipping, and dancing before the Lord. I rejoiced as God brought forth both understanding and revelation.

Every one of us has been called to the ministry in some way, either through the five-fold ministry gifts (apostle, prophet, evangelist, pastor, teacher), or to the ministry of helps somewhere in the local church. You can explore your ministry gifts in Romans 12; First Corinthians 12; and Ephesians 4. Nevertheless, we are ALL called by God to the ministry of reconciliation. We reconcile people to each other and to God through prayer and sharing of the gospel. Love is shed abroad in our hearts to the degree that the gifts people need from God flow out through us like a river reaching out to them. This divine force of love brings healing and restoration, imparting unto them all that they need so that there is nothing lacking. That is how the gifts should flow.

> *"Therefore My people shall know what My name is and what it means; therefore they shall know in that day that I am He who speaks; behold, I AM!*
>
> *How beautiful upon the mountains are the feet of him who brings good tidings, who publishes peace, who brings good tidings of good, who publishes salvation, who says to Zion, Your God reigns!*
>
> *Hark, your watchmen lift up their voices; together they sing for joy; for they shall see eye to eye the return of the Lord to Zion"* (Isaiah 52:6-8 AMP).

An intercessor is a watchman, that is, a person who is designated to guard something. The watchman fills in the gap, makes up the hedge, build up the walls. *"Together they shall sing for joy; for they shall see eye to eye,"* means that they will be united. They will stand with one mind, one heart, and one purpose.

There are two important things about unity the Lord showed me on May 8, 1980, as I was on a flight to Washington D.C. to minister. He led me to Ephesians 4:13.

> *"Till we all come in the unity of the faith, and of the knowledge of the Son of God, unto a perfect man, unto the measure of the stature of the fulness of Christ:"* (Ephesians 4:13).

The Lord showed me that there are two forces that come together, the unity of the Spirit, and the unity of the faith. He said to me, "Those two unite only through Me, and by My people yielding to it." The first being the unity of the Spirit, which can only be by His Holy Spirit, and then the unity of the faith in the knowledge of the Lord Jesus Christ, which is by the Word of Almighty God. He then told me that when these two unite, we have the unity of the glory.

The unity of Spirit and faith was evident in the latter part of the 20th century. In the latter half of the 1960's, there was a tremendous outpouring of the Spirit and many refer to it as the "Charismatic Renewal." It was remarkable because so many people from various mainline denominations were being baptized in the Holy Spirit and speaking in tongues. Among Catholics, this renewal began with students seeking the Lord at Duquesne University, and from there it spread powerfully until by the end of the 1970's, over a million Catholics were baptized in the Holy Spirit. This is only one of the many that were experiencing the outpouring of the Holy Spirit in this way.

Interestingly, this movement coincided with the 1967 Six Day War in Israel, where Jerusalem was restored to the nation of Israel. In 1967 also was the year of "Summer of Love," counterculture revolution where thousands of "hippies" poured into the Haight-Ashbury district of San Francisco. It was on the heels of race riots that forever changed our cities, Vietnam War protest demonstrations, and civil rights sit-ins. These were volatile times in the natural and powerful times in the Spirit. It was as if the natural and spiritual world were colliding and erupting simultaneously.

This outpouring of the Holy Spirit was followed by the Word of Faith movement where new emphasis was put on learning scripture and applying scripture by faith into everyday life. Both the Charismatic Renewal and the Word of Faith movements received great acceptance, but also great criticism from people who could not see beyond their comfort zone. When the Lord is doing a mighty work with His people, the enemy of our souls pours out vengeance and makes even greater effort to stop His will from being accomplished in the earth.

"...But where sin abounded, grace did much more abound:" (Romans 5:20).

We have the victory!

The Lord spoke to me concerning this and said, *"Just as they came against the Holy Spirit baptism, they have come against the Word of Faith, and will continue to come against it. However, they will not be able to squelch it, or put it out. It will grow stronger, and stronger, and stronger. There will be unity in the Spirit, and unity of faith, for the perfection, the maturity of the Body of Christ, that My work can be accomplished in the earth."* That is exactly what we are seeing being fulfilled in the church today. We are beginning to see eye to eye, and this increases in the lives of people who intercede.

House of Prayer

"Know ye not that ye are the temple of God, and that the Spirit of God dwelleth in you?" (1 Corinthians 3:16).

We are the temple of Almighty God. The temple is the house where God dwells, and it is also a place where He is worshipped, where prayer goes forth, and where great and mighty plans and purposes for eternity are laid. *"It is written, My house shall be called a house of prayer..."*

(Matthew 21:13). God no longer dwells in a temple of stone and metal, He dwells in His people, who are living temples. We are the house of prayer for all nations.

On the day of Pentecost, new dimensions of prayer came forth. As the believers were being baptized with the Holy Spirit and they spoke with other tongues, there was a miracle taking place among the hearers. Jerusalem was a cosmopolitan city even then and there were people from all parts of the known world.

> *"And they were all filled with the Holy Ghost, and began to speak with other tongues, as the Spirit gave them utterance.*
>
> *And there were dwelling at Jerusalem Jews, devout men, out of every nation under heaven.*
>
> *Now when this was noised abroad, the multitude came together, and were confounded, because that every man heard them speak in his own language"* *(Acts 2:4-6).*

Various people were hearing declarations about God in their own native tongues from Africa, Europe, and Asia.

> *"And how hear we every man in our own tongue, wherein we were born?*
>
> *Parthians, and Medes, and Elamites, and the dwellers in Mesopotamia, and in Judaea, and Cappadocia, in Pontus, and Asia,*

Phrygia, and Pamphylia, in Egypt, and in the parts of Libya about Cyrene, and strangers of Rome, Jews and proselytes,

Cretes and Arabians, we do hear them speak in our tongues the wonderful works of God" (Acts 2:8-11).

God clearly showed that He redeemed the descendents of Abraham, but didn't leave out the rest of humanity. This message of redemption was for all, as was the baptism in the Holy Spirit. The house of prayer is now available to all who believe, both Jew and Gentile, because as we become believers, we become His house of prayer.

This baptism of the Holy Spirit is for intercession and also for a sign to the unbeliever.

"Wherefore tongues are for a sign, not to them that believe, but to them that believe not: but prophesying serveth not for them that believe not, but for them which believes" (1 Corinthians 14:22).

Once I had received the baptism of the Holy Spirit, I had a desire to one day be praying in the Spirit, have someone recognize the words in their own language, and then interpret what was being spoken. My desire came to pass several times. Sometimes it is the language of the native land for believers. God speaks in their own language to reassure them of miraculous power for them.

This occurred in 1983 while I ministered in Guatemala. I led the people in intercession, praying in the spirit for seven straight hours. People were writing things on pads, and when I asked them what they were writing, they told me that they were writing the prophetic words I was saying in Spanish. I do not speak Spanish! I found out later that at the same time we were interceding, a coup d'état was averted, which would have been a blood bath. God was letting them know what to expect.

During my travels in Israel, I prayed for a couple who had come to Israel to negotiate the sale of helicopters. There were some difficulties in the transactions and I was asked to pray with the wife on behalf of these negotiations. After some time in intercession, she left. However, as she was leaving, she remarked to my hostess that she did not know I lived in Israel and was a Jewess. My hostess informed her that I didn't live in Israel, and that I am from the U.S.A. "*Well*," the woman said, "*she was speaking perfect Hebrew fluently. Where did she learn such perfect Hebrew?*"

"*Though she was speaking perfect Hebrew,*" came the reply, "*she was speaking in other tongues by the Holy Spirit.*"

The little daughter of the couple said, "*Yes, Mommy. She was speaking Hebrew. I heard her when I walked into the room. She said in Hebrew, 'Lord, bless the sale of those helicopters'.*" Now I have never learned Hebrew, but I was praying in other tongues as the Spirit of the Lord gave utterance, and it was a sign for the woman who needed to hear it.

This happened another time as I attended a Baptist church in Jerusalem. Someone asked me to pray for an eleven day old baby who weighed only two pounds. The mother of the child would not allow anyone to pray for her baby because she was prayed for and was never healed. This caused unbelief in her. The father of the child asked me to pray and I went into the nursery. When I saw the condition of the child, I was so glad to know that I serve a God of miracles. I began to praise God declaring that I knew what He wanted to do and that I knew His perfect will for that baby. I laid my hands on that tiny body and began to pray in the Holy Spirit. Instantly I knew that healing virtue had gone out of me into that infant. I thanked God and praised Him. The father stood next to me, and after I finished I looked at him staring at me in amazement. He leaned over and asked, *"Do you know what language you were praying in?"*

I responded that I didn't and he replied, *"I did not think you did. You were praying in the language of my wife's church. She is Russian, and Russian Orthodox. I go with her to church. You were praying in the same language they use in prayer at our Russian Orthodox church. That language is the high language of Russia, like the Queen's English is the high language of England. It is Slavonic, and you were praying in perfect Slavonic."*

The mother of the child stepped in between us and wept uncontrollably. The father asked her if she heard what I was praying over the child. She acknowledged that she did, and I told her that her baby is whole. She then agreed and said that she did agree because she heard me say in Slavonic, *"You are healed by the stripes of Jesus."* Today that child has grown to be a healthy and whole human being. The mother is no longer a doubter, but rather a believer in the Name of Jesus. It was a sign to the unbeliever that produced a miracle for the baby and the mother.

Another time my prayer in the Spirit was in Spanish. I was praying for missionaries who needed prayer for emotional hurts that were inflicted upon them. As I prayed for the woman, I said to the Lord, *"Lord, this hurt has to go. She cannot be an effective minister with that hurt. Lord, heal her."* Then I began to speak in tongues while inside I was saying, *"Lord, love her through me. Let my arms be Your arms and, let them be light, life and love to completely heal that wound in her."*

Afterwards, her husband asked me if I knew what I was saying. I answered that I didn't. He said, *"You were* saying, *'to give a hug, to give a hug' in Spanish.*" His wife was totally delivered and made free that day through the power of intercession.

Another time I was teaching on intercession in Ballston Spa, New York. There was a Greek Orthodox couple in the congregation and they had come to the meeting because they noticed an advertisement on a downtown storefront window. After teaching the Word, many people came to the front for prayer. As I laid my hands on each one, I prayed in both English and in tongues as the Spirit of the Lord led me. While the glory of the Lord was still ministering to the people, I returned to the platform and I noticed this couple looking at me in astonishment. I perceived in my spirit that they had never experienced anything like they were feeling and seeing.

I went to them and in conversation, the man said, *"I did not know you are Greek."* I laughed and said that I'm not Greek. He then asked me where I learned to speak fluent Greek. I explained that it was by the Holy Spirit. The Holy Spirit knows what each one needs to have faith increased, including signs and wonders.

Strengthening Your Spirit

Intercession will develop your spirit. In the same manner that the Word of God renews your mind, the Holy Spirit develops your spirit as you yield to Him. Hunger and thirst in the body decreases physical strength. It is the same in the spirit of man. Hunger and thirst for lack of the Word of God and the Holy Spirit diminishes strength and then we grow weak and faint. Then we will not accomplish the work of the ministry. The Lord used Isaiah 44 to reveal to me that a balanced life in the study of the Word of God along with the communion of the Holy Spirit is necessary to accomplish all that He has for us.

> *"The smith with the tongs both worketh in the coals, and fashioneth it with hammers, and worketh it with the strength of his arms: yea, he is hungry, and his strength faileth: he drinketh no water, and is faint"* *(Isaiah 44:12).*

When I think of strength, I am reminded of Paul Anderson. He was from my home town of Toccoa, Georgia, and lived about two blocks from where I grew up. His family attended the same church as mine. Paul was a great football player, and began developing his weight lifting ability as a teenager. He went on to Furman University, but what he began in the small town of Toccoa, Georgia, took him all the way to the Olympics. In 1956, he won the Gold Medal in weight lifting and was declared the World's Strongest Man.

As I envisioned Paul Anderson's great physical strength, the Lord showed me that as strong as he was, his strength would be useless if he fainted. I thought about how many Christians are strong in the Word, having developed a great deal of knowledge about scripture. However, if they don't drink the water of the Holy Spirit, they grow weary and faint.

> *"For with stammering lips and another tongue will he speak to this people.*
>
> *To whom he said, This is the rest wherewith ye may cause the weary to rest; and this is the refreshing: yet they would not hear"* *(Isaiah 28:11,12).*

The Greek word for faint and weary is *kopos*. It means *labor, a beating, to toil, trouble or vexation.* This is the way the Body of Christ becomes when they do not pray in the Spirit. They are vexed with little problems and lack the strength to deal with troubles. So many are overwhelmed and then become immobilized because they don't drink of the living waters of the Holy Spirit.

"Hungry and thirsty, their soul fainted in them" (Psalm 107:5).

In this verse, the Hebrew word for fainted is *ataph*, and the prime root of the word means *to shroud or clothe*. In this sense the idea is that hunger and thirst causes the soul to languish; to be covered over like a shroud; to fail; to be feeble; to hide; to be overwhelmed; to swoon. It portrays a picture of a shriveled up person lacking the energy to do anything. That is what happens when we don't pray. Darkness (ignorance) covers over our real self, the spirit man.

The promise of the Holy Spirit guiding us into all truth (John 16:13) becomes limited, and the rest and refreshing (Isaiah 28: 12) is missing. We are told to hold fast to the Word committed to us, but without the Holy Spirit, that cannot happen. The Word of God is life and health (Proverbs 4:20-23) in every area of our lives.

"Pay attention, my child, to what I say. Listen carefully. Don't lose sight of my words. Let them penetrate deep within your heart, for they bring life and radiant health to anyone who discovers their meaning. Above all else, guard your heart, for it affects everything you do" (Proverbs 4:20-23 NLT).

The word *keep* in Second Timothy 1:14 is *phulasso* in Greek, meaning *to guard, watch, keep watch, to keep by the way of protection*. This is exactly what intercessors do. They are watchmen as the Holy Spirit of peace sets up a garrison of protection around the heart and as He takes a personal interest in the action.

"Wherefore I put thee in remembrance that thou stir up the gift of God, which is in thee by the putting on of my hands.

For God hath not given us the spirit of fear; but of power, and of love, and of a sound mind" (2 Timothy 6,7).

"For the which cause I also suffer these things: nevertheless I am not ashamed: for I know whom I have believed, and am persuaded that he is able to keep that which I have committed unto him against that day.

Hold fast the form of sound words, which thou hast heard of me, in faith and love which is in Christ Jesus.

That good thing which was committed unto thee keep by the Holy Ghost which dwelleth in us" (2 Timothy 1:12-14).

As we pray in the spirit, we breathe life into the Body of Christ. We bring the life of God through healing, prosperity, miracles, and through every way necessary to bring wholeness to His people.

"He that believeth on me, as the scripture hath said, out of his belly shall flow rivers of living water" (John 7:38).

Weariness is replaced by refreshing when we pray in the Spirit. Then the Word can go forth in power so that we can be blessed and be a blessing.

"Never return evil for evil or insult for insult (scolding, tongue-lashing, berating), but on the contrary blessing [praying for their welfare, happiness, and protection, and truly pitying and loving them]. For know that to this you have been called, that you may yourselves inherit a blessing [from God—that you may obtain a blessing as heirs, bringing welfare and happiness and protection]" (1 Peter 3:9 AMP).

Look Beyond

Look Beyond

"Turn your eyes upon Jesus
Look full in His wonderful face
And the things of earth will grow strangely dim,
In the light of His glory and grace."
— Helen Howarth Lemmel

These famous beautiful lyrics are from a song published in 1922 by Helen H. Lemmel (1864-1961). Her prolific work includes over 500 songs and poems that are included in many hymnals. Upon reading a tract (booklet) that deeply impressed her, she composed this song. She stated, *"Suddenly, as if commanded to stop and listen, I stood still, and singing in my soul and spirit was the chorus, with not one conscious moment of putting word to word to make rhyme, or note to note to make melody. The verses were written the same week, after the usual manner of composition, but nonetheless dictated by the Holy Spirit."* The lyrics of this song continue to bless worshippers more that 80 years after they were published, because the truth of these words is eternal.

"Yea doubtless, and I count all things but loss for the excellency of the knowledge of Christ Jesus my Lord: for whom I have suffered the loss of all things, and do count them but dung, that I may win Christ,

And be found in him, not having mine own righteousness, which is of the law, but that which is through the faith of Christ, the righteousness which is of God by faith:

That I may know him, and the power of his resurrection, and the fellowship of his sufferings, being made conformable unto his death;

If by any means I might attain unto the resurrection of the dead" (Philippians 3:7-11).

Knowing Him is the center of it all. Earthly knowledge is good, but it can never compare with the intimate knowledge of Him. Just claiming membership in the Body of Christ is not enough. There are those who use the jargon of Christianity, but never really get to **know** Him. It takes a lot more than "talking the talk" to "walk the walk." It takes relationship, and that means time spent in His presence. This is the essence of Helen Lemmel's lyrics and the essence of the intercessor's close walk with Jesus.

The Mountain of God

Several stories in the Bible tell of the mountain of the Lord, the mount of God, or the holy mountain. It refers to a high place where God has had divine visitation with mankind. In these stories, God brought divine order, structure, and laws resulting in change.

Abraham was instructed to take his beloved son Isaac to a mountain (Mount Moriah) and offer him as a sacrifice. At the point of raising the knife to accomplish this unimaginably hard task, an angel was sent to stop his arm and an animal was provided for the sacrifice. This event made a change for the seed of Abraham. There was no doubt about Abraham's obedience to God, and the blessings that would belong to his seed forever. Redemption was to come from the sacrifice of a perfect son. Jesus was crucified on Calvary, which is part of the Moriah mountain chain, and He became the instrument of redemption for all mankind. Because of

His sacrifice, we are grafted into the seed of Abraham and receive the blessings.

When Moses received the tablets of the Ten Commandments, he was called to Mount Sinai to be alone with God. He received the law for the nation of Israel that set the standard of righteousness living for the nation until the coming of Messiah. The nation of Israel was changed from a loose confederation of people with common lineage to a nation with purpose having one law and one God.

Elijah, the prophet, dealt with the prophets of Baal on Mount Carmel. This remarkable story forever declared that the idols and false gods had no power. This miraculous event changed the political leadership of the nation as it exposed the evil of Jezebel and her priests. Idol worship frequently took place on the "high places" following the pattern of the Tower of Babel where men attempted to reach heaven by their own strength. Even cultures not mentioned in the Bible including the Inca, Aztec, Olmec, Khmer, and others, have high places of idol worship. It is the counterfeit of establishing a high place where the one true God meets with mankind in divine visitation.

Jesus was transfigured into the ultimate glory on the Mount of Transfiguration, joined by Moses and Elijah. That which was in Him was no longer hidden by His physical body. Those who were with Him saw the Son of Glory in all His fullness and were forever changed. It gives us the hope of glory knowing that as He is, so shall we be.

That is the way it is even now. Whenever God brings us to a "mountain" of visitation in intercession, He is about to bring change to our lives. We are symbolically standing on the edge of a great mountain where the winds of His Spirit are blowing on the coals of the divine altar, fanning the flames of the coming revival. Visitation always produces change in us and in our circumstances.

You Are Well Able to Take the Land

More than anything, I want to encourage you. There is so much more beyond the horizon for the church than what can be seen by the naked eye. The glorious destiny of the church is beyond human imagination and it welcomes all who want to join it. It requires a people of vision, persistence, and courage.

There is a familiar story we learned in elementary school about a man who had great vision, courage, and determination. He could see beyond his peers, and beyond criticism. He was not afraid to take risks and he envisioned what seemed to others an impossible dream. That dream set him on a course with historic destiny. This visionary was Christopher Columbus, whose story still serves to inspire and encourage the young. Columbus said, *"Nothing that results from human progress is achieved with unanimous consent. And those who are enlightened before the others are doomed to pursue that light, in spite of others."*

Some onlookers, gazing into the sunset, might have thought Columbus was on a fool's errand. They were dream killers. They had no vision. We also know people of that sort, and just being around them drains your spirit. Instead of lifting up your arms, they have their hands clasped around your ankles. We need to refrain from listening to people like that. History records the success of the 1492 voyage of Columbus and its pivotal impact for generations to come.

Dream killers are like the ten out of the twelve spies who reported back to the wilderness camp of Israel about the Promised Land (Numbers 13-14). They reported that the

Promised Land they were about to enter had giants and the Israelites were like grasshoppers by comparison. Only two of the spies, Joshua and Caleb, came back with words of encouragement, declaring that it was a land of milk and honey and that they were well able to take the land.

Do you have a vision? Do you have it for your family? Do you have it for your nation? Can you see what lies beyond the veil of your natural sight? Many people think that intercessors have "fallen off the edge of the world" like the critics of Columbus and that they are on a fool's errand. Intercession is a place for pursuing and expanding visions, dreams, and destiny. Keep on sailing!

It is not hard to imagine the watchmen on the shoreline of Spain looking out onto the horizon. First they see one ship, then the second, then the third, coming from seemingly nowhere passing the sign above the Straits of Gibraltar that says, *"Ne Plus Ultra"* (Nothing Beyond). Columbus proved that there is more beyond. The sign needed to be changed to "Plus Ultra" (More Beyond). So it is with intercession.

Intercessors go beyond that which can be seen with the natural eye. They believe beyond, see beyond, and reach beyond. They have the courage to keep pressing forward, never becoming so frustrated that they give up. We may be fulfilling the visions of some past generations who did not see the fulfillment of their visions and dreams come to pass. Let us pray that more visions, destinies, and dreams come to pass.

Intercessors see beyond that which is natural into the supernatural. Even though the video and press media or other resources may be used to bring understanding about events and issues, people who pray don't necessarily rely on them. They know for themselves what God is saying, and that is enough. They have hope where there is no hope. They see beyond the veil of flesh. They become the trumpets of the Most High God, decreeing, declaring, and prophesying to the wind according to the direction of the Holy Spirit.

> *"Wherefore seeing we also are compassed about with so great a cloud of witnesses, let us lay aside every weight, and the sin which doth so easily beset us, and let us run with patience the race that is set before us,*
>
> *Looking unto Jesus the author and finisher of our faith; who for the joy that was set before him endured the cross, despising the shame, and is set down at the right hand of the throne of God"* *(Hebrews 12:1,2).*

Now and then I imagine a "cloud of witnesses" looking down over the banister of heaven cheering us on and shouting, *"Go for it! You can make it!"*

Who is He?

Settling the central question of "Who is Jesus?" is at the very core of our belief, and from that rock of revelation all things go forth, including the confidence of intercession. The disciples of Jesus were confronted with this simple, yet profound question.

> *"When Jesus came into the coasts of Caesarea Philippi, he asked his disciples, saying, Whom do men say that I the Son of man am?*

And they said, Some say that thou art John the Baptist: some, Elias; and others, Jeremias, or one of the prophets.

He saith unto them, But whom say ye that I am?

And Simon Peter answered and said, Thou art the Christ, the Son of the living God.

And Jesus answered and said unto him, Blessed art thou, Simon Barjona: for flesh and blood hath not revealed it unto thee, but my Father which is in heaven.

And I say also unto thee, That thou art Peter, and upon this rock I will build my church; and the gates of hell shall not prevail against it" (Matthew 16:13-18).

These followers left their homes, possessions, families, and careers to follow this man from Galilee. He was a carpenter's son, whose hands probably had evidence of a fine craftsman. They watched Him lay those hands on the blind, deaf, and diseased, and saw the miraculous healings, even raising people from the dead. They heard him command the wind and the sea into obedience, and watched Him walk on water. Even so, who was He? Who was He to them? Finally, Simon Peter responded correctly about who He is, as well as what His mission was. He is the Son of God, and the Anointed One (Christ) Who is the promised Messiah and Redeemer.

The response from Jesus (Matthew 16:17,18) still resonates in the church today. This "rock" is the personal revelation of Who Jesus Christ really is. It begins with knowing that He is the Son of God, and that He is our personal Messiah. More revelation about Who He is comes with personal intimacy, experiences, and knowledge of Him. You can only do that by studying the Word and in prayer.

In Matthew 16:18, Jesus is speaking about His church prevailing over the gates of hell, meaning to be victorious. People who prevail are those who have a personal revelation of Who Jesus is. This revelation does not come from the natural mind, but from God. Until we receive the revelation of the person of Jesus Christ, Whose we are and Whom we serve, we will not prevail against the gates of hell. You can pray until your knees are worn out and confess until you wear out your confessor, but those prayers will not avail much. How can the church hope to see the glory of the Lord without knowing Him?

The fundamental belief that must be established is that Jesus came and died for us. From there we grow into understanding His plans and purposes for each of us. He gives us staying power, delivering power, and victory as we pursue those plans and purposes. When storms of life come to steal your vision, you have the supernatural power to stand because you stand in the power and glory of Almighty God. Jesus is the Christ, the Son of the living God in you. He is your hope and the anchor of your soul.

> *"What? know ye not that your body is the temple of the Holy Ghost which is in you, which ye have of God, and ye are not your own?" (1 Corinthians 6:19).*

This revelation does not come with half-hearted or careless thought. It comes to those who are committed to Him and His will for their lives; to those who have surrendered "all" to God!

One Day, One Step at a Time

I was baptized in the Holy Spirit on September 21, 1969. I became so close to the Father, and knew that He had something for me to do. Consequently, I cried out to the Lord to show me His will for my life. I said, *"Show me what You want me to do, Lord. Whatever it is, I will do it."* This heart's cry went on for nine months in prayer, fasting, and weeping before the Lord. By this time I had become the organist for Evangel Temple in Columbus, Georgia, where the pastor and his wife lovingly mentored me in the Word and things of the Holy Spirit.

On a Sunday morning in May, 1970, the presence of God came into the sanctuary in such a powerful way that the pastor invited the congregation to come forward to the altar and kneel before the Lord. Everyone found their way forward and before long, they were in deep communion with God, weeping and glorifying Him. There is nothing better than being in the presence of Jesus and telling Him all about your concerns.

There is a place in your heart where you alone meet with God. It is the place where you hide all of your deepest secrets, where mortar is mixed to build the wall that we like to hide behind. This is the portion that needs to be rescued by Him, and where He beckons us to come. He has proved Himself to be the God that really knows each of us.

"O Lord, thou hast searched me, and known me.

Thou knowest my downsitting and mine uprising, thou understandest my thought afar off.

Thou compassest my path and my lying down, and art acquainted with all my ways.

For there is not a word in my tongue, but, lo, O LORD, thou knowest it altogether.

Thou hast beset me behind and before, and laid thine hand upon me.

Such knowledge is too wonderful for me; it is high, I cannot attain unto it.

Whither shall I go from thy spirit? or whither shall I flee from thy presence?

If I ascend up into heaven, thou art there: if I make my bed in hell, behold, thou art there.

If I take the wings of the morning, and dwell in the uttermost parts of the sea;

Even there shall thy hand lead me, and thy right hand shall hold me.

If I say, Surely the darkness shall cover me; even the night shall be light about me.

Yea, the darkness hideth not from thee; but the night shineth as the day: the darkness and the light are both alike to thee.

For thou hast possessed my reins: thou hast covered me in my mother's womb.

I will praise thee; for I am fearfully and wonderfully made: marvellous are thy works; and that my soul knoweth right well.

My substance was not hid from thee, when I was made in secret, and curiously wrought in the lowest parts of the earth.

Thine eyes did see my substance, yet being unperfect; and in thy book all my members were written, which in continuance were fashioned, when as yet there was none of them.

How precious also are thy thoughts unto me, O God! how great is the sum of them!

If I should count them, they are more in number than the sand: when I awake, I am still with thee.

...Search me, O God, and know my heart: try me, and know my thoughts:

And see if there be any wicked way in me, and lead me in the way everlasting" *(Psalm 139:1-18, 23-24).*

On that Sunday morning in May, I sat at the organ bench until I just had to move and kneel before the Lord as the others were doing. I walked to the front pew and fell to my knees weeping and repeating the prayer, *"Jesus, please tell me what it is You want me to do, and I promise, I will do it."* As I was praying, I lost all sense of time, and I don't exactly know how long I was there. Between tearful pleas, I heard a sweet voice of a 65 year old woman whisper into my right ear, *"Jesus, just tell her Your will for her life is to follow You, one day, one step at a time".* 2/27/09

That was all I heard, no more or less. Like arrows, those words shot straight to my heart. I realized that I didn't have to know where I would go, nor be concerned about who

He wanted me to be. All I would need to do is to follow Jesus, one day, one step at a time.

When I opened my eyes and dried my tears, I looked around the sanctuary and found that everyone had left. Then I looked toward the foyer and my eyes met the pastor's mother standing there. She walked towards me and I met her half way, thinking to myself that she was the one who whispered in my ear. I wanted to thank her and when I told her about what I heard, she said, *"I haven't been praying with you. You have been in here for a long time all by yourself."*

Even though there was no one there, I know I distinctly heard that woman's voice. Those anointed words penetrated the depths of my soul. I asked the Lord whose words they were and He responded, *"It is the voice of a 65 year old woman in Romania praying in other tongues – English!"* The Holy Spirit brought her prayers all the way from Romania to Columbus, Georgia. Many times I reflect on her gentle anointed words and they guide me still. That is prophetic intercession.

Thirteen years later, I was at a conference in California. A minister I knew recognized me and came across the room to greet me. He was nearly bursting with excitement to tell me what happened that year. He had been on a mission trip to an Eastern European nation that was under Communist control at the time. He was smuggling my intercessory prayer teaching tapes to give to pastors who frequently were imprisoned for their faith. He told me that they desperately needed to learn how to pray in the Spirit and have the revelation that was on the Intercessory Prayer teaching series. They needed to learn how to stay out of prison so that they could pastor their people.

Several sets of my teaching cassette tapes were packed into his briefcase, which were forbidden and should have been confiscated. As the border guards began searching through his things, they grabbed his briefcase, opened it, and examined the tapes. Then they simply returned them to the briefcase and commanded him to go. Either God blinded the eyes of the border guards, or they knew precisely what they were doing. God used him and the border guards to safely take my intercessory prayer tapes into **Romania**. Hallelujah!

It is incredible when you think about how a small moment of your life could become so meaningful. Most of these moments pass so quickly, but they cast a beam of light on the future, and make them unforgettable. I will never forget the precious woman from Romania who selflessly spent time in intercession for me. God raised me up to teach His Body on intercession and those very teachings went to her own nation helping to set Romanians free. If she is still living, she would be over 100 years old. Unless God showed her, she may have never known what God did with her prayers, but I know and she will find out in heaven. I am eternally grateful.

Saints, the walk of faith and knowing Jesus is the grandest walk you will know in your life. Even though a life of intercession does cost the flesh, what price could you put on souls? When you know Him, every day of your life becomes an adventure. The lyrics of an old song still tell it so well.

He is my everything; He is my all.

He is my everything, both great and small.

He gave His life for me, made everything new.

He is my everything; He'll satisfy you.

Jesus is the Christ, Son of the Living God!

Sufficient Grace

We receive everything from the Lord according to our earnest expectations and hope. The hope we have is not a natural hope, but it is rested and centered on the Word of God and in the person of Jesus Christ, our only hope and glory. Within and among us as a Body, we carry this hope of realizing the glory of God in the here and now, not only the hereafter.

> *"Even the mystery which hath been hid from ages and from generations, but now is made manifest to his saints:*
>
> *To whom God would make known what is the riches of the glory of this mystery among the Gentiles; which is Christ in you, the hope of glory:*
>
> *Whom we preach, warning every man, and teaching every man in all wisdom; that we may present every man perfect in Christ Jesus:" (Colossians 1:26-28).*

All that we are, or ever hope to be is by the grace of God. The meanings of *grace* include *to indue with special honor; to be acceptable; to be highly favored.* As believers, we have been indued with special honor. We are accepted in the beloved and are highly favored.

> *"But by the grace of God I am what I am: and his grace which was bestowed upon me was not in vain; but I laboured more abundantly than they all: yet not I, but the grace of God which was with me" (1 Corinthians 15:10).*

If we truly believe that His grace is with us, then we must remain focused on Jesus, Who is our hope of glory. By Him, we are able ministers, not in our own sufficiency, but in the sufficiency of Almighty God. Our own strength and resources are not enough for the spirit-led life. However, through Christ, we are fully equipped.

> *"And such trust have we through Christ to God-ward:*
>
> *Not that we are sufficient of ourselves to think any thing as of ourselves; but our sufficiency is of God;*
>
> *Who also hath made us able ministers of the new testament; not of the letter, but of the spirit: for the letter killeth, but the spirit giveth life" (2 Corinthians 3:4-6).*

Jesus makes us fully functional to do the work of the ministry of reconciliation.

Spirit and Power

Jesus' disciples recognized that He has supernatural strength and ability. They also recognized that they would need the same operating in them in order to do the ministry of Christ in the earth.

> *"And it came to pass, that, as he was praying in a certain place, when he ceased, one of his disciples said unto him, Lord, teach us to pray, as John also taught his disciples" (Luke 11:1).*

This passage is so interesting, not only because of what it says, but its implications for us today. Why would the disciples of Jesus ask Him how to pray? Had they not heard anyone praying before? Was prayer a new concept? They indeed were familiar with ritual prayer in the synagogues, but this was something beyond ritual. They recognized that the nature of prayer that Jesus prayed is the secret to walking in the power and glory of Almighty God. As they watched Jesus as closely as they did, they saw that this Man's prayer life produced power and complete success. They also figured out that they needed to be taught about the prayer life that produced the kind of walk that Jesus walked.

Matthew 28:18 says that all power in heaven and earth has been given to Jesus, and in Luke 9, it further says that Jesus gave this power to His disciples. We have been given this awesome power, but we are responsible to find out how it operates and to use it to advance the kingdom of heaven.

Everything we do for the kingdom is fueled by the power of God. His efficient working in us gives us the ability to overcome spiritual inertia and get things accomplished in prayer and ministry. The Greek word *energeia*, from which the word energy is derived, means *efficient supernatural working power*. This word describes God's mighty power working in us and through us.

> *"And what is the exceeding greatness of his power to us-ward who believe, according to the <u>working</u> of his mighty power," (Ephesians 1:19).*

> *"Whereof I was made a minister, according to the gift of the grace of God given unto me by the effectual <u>working</u> of his power" (Ephesians 3:7).*

It is nothing less than the energy of Almighty God working in us.

Among the many words for power in Greek, there are two that are found in over 100 scripture verses in the New Testament, *exousia* and *dunamis*. *Exousia* means *privilege in force, capacity, competency, freedom, or mastery; delegated influence in authority, jurisdiction, liberty, power, right, or strength*. It is best to see this word in context to understand that this word tells us that Jesus was given all authority and has given us the authority to use His Name to accomplish His works in and through us.

> *"And Jesus came and spake unto them, saying, All power is given unto me in heaven and in earth" (Matthew 28:18).*

> *"For though he was crucified through weakness, yet he liveth by the power of God. For we also are weak in him, but we shall live with him by the power of God toward you" (2 Corinthians 13:4).*

Dunamis is the other Greek word that means *to have ability, abundance, mighty miracle power, strength, violent power*. The word dynamite is derived from it. This is the power that is imparted when one receives the baptism of the Holy Spirit.

> *"But ye shall receive power, after that the Holy Ghost is come upon you: and ye shall be witnesses unto me both in Jerusalem, and in all Judaea, and in Samaria, and unto the uttermost part of the earth" (Acts 1:8).*

It is the explosive power of God to work mighty miracles, to do all that He calls us to do, and accomplish the works that build the kingdom of heaven.

"And what is the exceeding greatness of his power to us-ward who believe, according to the working of his mighty power," (Ephesians 1:19).

"Now unto him that is able to do exceeding abundantly above all that we ask or think, according to the power that worketh in us," (Ephesians 3:20).

We have the confident assurance that God is not only interested in our lives, but has infused us with His power to accomplish our destinies in Him.

I discovered something about chickens that has served as a metaphor for understanding the miracle working *"dunamis"* power in us. Inside a hen, there is a sac that holds eggs. They vary in size from microscopic ones to the full sized egg that it is about to lay. It reminds me of *dunamis* miracles in that we have miracles in our spirits waiting to be "hatched." As we come in contact with someone who needs a miracle, we have the miracle working power within and this power of the Holy Spirit works through us.

As conditions of faith are met, we see these miracles happen. There is no limit or end to the Holy Spirit. Therefore, as we walk in faith and keep *"...building up yourselves on your most holy faith, praying in the Holy Ghost," (Jude 20)*, we will not find a limit or end to the miracles that are waiting to come forth and be a blessing to someone.

The account of Jesus in the wilderness is an example of the Spirit and power working together. Right after He was baptized in the Jordan River where the Holy Spirit descended upon Him, He was led into the wilderness.

"And he was there in the wilderness forty days, tempted of Satan; and was with the wild beasts; and the angels ministered unto him" (Mark 1:13).

He spent forty days fasting and praying in a most desolate place becoming spiritually fortified, and then had the notable encounter with Satan. His flesh was put in subjection to His Spirit as He spent those days in intercession. When He encountered the demonic powers, they were no match for Him. He came out of the wilderness and *"...returned in the power of the Spirit into Galilee..."* (Luke 4:14). Jesus went into the wilderness filled with the Holy Spirit into a season of heavy intercession and temptation. He came out of the wilderness in the power (*dunamis*) of the Holy Spirit. Power, anointing, the glory – these are what praying in the Holy Spirit will produce in a yielded life.

Fighting Beasts

In Mark 1:33, it says that Jesus was with the wild beasts in the wilderness. In the Judean desert, there are indeed, literal wild beasts and no doubt that added to the distressful conditions of spending so much time there alone. However, another meaning of beasts (*therion* in Greek) metaphorically, is *a brutal, bestial being that is savage and ferocious*. In the spirit realm, Jesus dealt with beings that fit this description and so do we. The apostle Paul writes,

"For we wrestle not against flesh and blood, but against principalities, against powers, against the rulers of the darkness of this world, against spiritual wickedness in high places" (Ephesians 6:12).

These powers and rulers of darkness are the beasts of the spirit world.

The Lord once gave me a vivid demonstration of the principle of fighting wild beasts as I was ministering on intercession in Thomaston, Georgia. During the sermon, I heard the Holy Spirit tell me to call the pastor and his wife forward to the front. I obeyed and so did they.

Then the Holy Spirit told me to call the elders of the church to form a circle around the pastor and his wife. I obeyed and so did they. Once more, the Holy Spirit instructed me to call the members of the congregation to form a circle around the elders. Again, I obeyed and so did they. Finally, the Holy Spirit had me call forth the visitors to the church to encircle the church members.

By this time, my curiosity about these concentric circles overtook my mind and I asked the Lord, *"Would you mind letting me in on what we are doing?"*

The Lord answered, *"Turn to Acts 14 and read verses 19 and 20 then you will know what you are doing."*

I located the scriptures and read aloud.

"And there came thither certain Jews from Antioch and Iconium, who persuaded the people, and having stoned Paul, drew him out of the city, supposing he had been dead.

Howbeit, as the disciples stood round about him, he rose up, and came into the city: and the next day he departed with Barnabas to Derbe" (Acts 14:19,20).

As I read, the revelation of what was happening and what the Lord was showing us just exploded. The Lord said,

"Ask the elders what they would do if they saw wild beasts coming to attack their pastor and his wife and family." Likewise, He instructed me to ask each outer circle the same question. Clearly, we all would do everything within our power to prevent such a thing from happening.

The Holy Spirit revealed that just as Jesus and the apostle Paul fought with the wild beasts, the same demonic forces were coming to attack this pastor and his family, and subsequently all who are associated with him. The Lord gave me and the congregation further explanation about this. He directed my attention to Acts 14, where the disciples stood around Paul. He then asked, *"Do you think these apostles, who were filled with My dunamis power, were standing around Paul in despair? No. When they formed a circle around Paul, they formed a circle of life. Paul had no choice but to rise up well and whole in the newness of resurrection life. He was to go forth and forward to complete his call."* We all rejoiced in this revelation. When each person prays for the other in the Spirit, a circle of life forms a wall of protection around them preventing such forces from fulfilling their assignments.

Strengthened With Might

As you read the four Gospels, you get a vivid picture of just how much time Jesus spent in prayer. In some places you read where Jesus prayed all night long. He spent much time with the Father so that He could do what He saw His Father doing. He was strengthened by spending time with God in order to walk in total obedience to the Father's will and do the mighty works that He did. The apostle Paul prayed for the Ephesians for this strengthening.

"That he would grant you, according to the riches of his glory, to be strengthened with might by his Spirit in the inner man;" (Ephesians 3:16).

This prayer is for believers today. When we pray in the Holy Spirit, Almighty God strengthens us in our inner beings. Proverbs 4:22 tells us that His Words are life and strength to us, and health to our flesh. As we are obedient to God and His Word, praying in the Holy Spirit, and worshipping Him, we will experience the supernatural *dunamis*, the dynamite power of the Holy Spirit. It is the power and anointing in which Jesus walked.

Circumcised Lips

It is equally important to know that walking in the power and authority of Almighty God is in the power of what we say. The Lord revealed this to me in a very peculiar way. I was counseling a woman over the phone when before I realized the impact of what I was saying, I told her, *"We are going to agree that they will have circumcised lips, and will not speak negatively concerning this issue for which they are praying."*

I had no idea of the severity of what I had just said. I only knew by the witness in my spirit that I had spoken the Word of the Lord. After my conversation with the woman, I went to the Lord in prayer about this. I began to wonder and said to the Lord, *"Lord, you must tell me what circumcised lips are, so that I will know what I am agreeing for."*

He led me to Genesis 17:14, where Abraham was given instructions regarding circumcision and that it was to be a token of God's covenant with Abraham and his seed. Circumcision is a cutting away of the flesh. To the Israelites, this means a consecration to God and keeping a blood covenant with Him and His blessings. Today it is a common practice in hospitals for the purpose of cleanliness. Most recently, the World Health Organization announced findings that men who are circumcised are significantly less likely to contract or spread AIDS. Aren't God's ways amazing!

The Lord said to me, *"When My people circumcise their tongues, they are entering into a covenant of life. Speaking negatively only brings death and negates covenant blessings. The tongue is the instrument of spirit life which results in covenant blessings in your spirit, soul, and body."*

"Death and life are in the power of the tongue: and they that love it shall eat the fruit thereof" (Proverbs 18:21).

If there is anything that will literally stop the flow of anointing and the power of Almighty God quicker than anything else, it is having uncircumcised lips. This includes negative speaking, which is saying the opposite of what God says in the Word. It also includes all unrighteous criticism, judgments, backbiting, gossip, and other works of the flesh through the spoken word. These acts will bring the effectiveness of prayers to a screeching halt.

As intercessors, we have to make a covenant with God about our lips. It is not a literal cutting, but we must "circumcise" our speech so that His will can be accomplished through us. Circumcised lips speak in agreement with God and His Word, regardless of what the circumstances are. We must be careful to guard what we say about the situations we have entrusted into prayer. We must guard ourselves in giving opinions and criticisms that are harmful. When we are watchful over our words, we can have the full assurance of the promise found in Romans 8.

"Likewise the Spirit also helpeth our infirmities: for we know not what we should pray for as we ought: but the Spirit itself maketh intercession for us with groanings which cannot be uttered.

And he that searcheth the hearts knoweth what is the mind of the Spirit, because he maketh intercession for the saints according to the will of God.

And we know that all things work together for good to them that love God, to them who are the called according to his purpose" (Romans 8:26-28).

The Object of God's Love

To even scratch the surface of understanding the love of God for mankind, we may look to the beginning where His love for fallen mankind was first expressed. The treachery of Adam and Eve required the justice of a righteous God. Nevertheless, the God of love added mercy for mankind by the promise of a Redeemer, Who would bring salvation to a lost world.

Generations later, God gave His promise of a son and innumerable descendents to Abraham, one of which would be the Redeemer of all mankind (Genesis 12:3). God's love extended to all humanity.

"And the scripture, foreseeing that God would justify the heathen through faith, preached before the gospel unto Abraham, saying, In thee shall all nations be blessed" (Galatians 3:8).

When God provided the sacrifice of the ram to replace Isaac on Mount Moriah, God repeated the blessings of Abraham, his seed, and all the nations through him. He swore His oath of blessings by Himself because there was no higher power to swear by. This meant that if God had not brought this promise to pass, He would cease to exist. That would also mean the end of the entire universe because He holds it together. The promise was sealed by a blood sacrifice indicating a covenant that would not be broken.

This act of God became an anchor to Abraham's soul. Abraham and his descendants needed the promise of redemption and the token of God's oath (the blood sacrifice) to hold onto until the Redeemer comes.

> *"But, beloved, we are persuaded better things of you, and things that accompany salvation, though we thus speak.*
>
> *For God is not unrighteous to forget your work and labour of love, which ye have shewed toward his name, in that ye have ministered to the saints, and do minister.*
>
> *And we desire that every one of you do shew the same diligence to the full assurance of hope unto the end:*
>
> *That ye be not slothful, but followers of them who through faith and patience inherit the promises.*
>
> *For when God made promise to Abraham, because he could swear by no greater, he sware by himself," (Hebrews 6:9-13).*

The act of love that God displayed toward Abraham caused him to believe God and His Word. God credited

Abraham's belief as righteousness, as He did for all who came after Abraham and believed the covenant promise.

When the fullness of time was at hand, Jesus fulfilled the promise of redemption and again exhibited the great love of God.

> *"For God so loved the world, that he gave his only begotten Son, that whosoever believeth in him should not perish, but have everlasting life" (John 3:16).*

We cannot fully comprehend just how much God desires the redemption of His people, His beloved creation. Salvation is such an amazing act of the Divine.

Without God, we are in darkness and without hope. We hardly even know that we need a Savior, *"Because the carnal mind is enmity against God: for it is not subject to the law of God, neither indeed can be" (Romans 8:7).* God reached out to humanity even when we were clueless as to how much we needed Him.

Image of Christ

First John tells us that Jesus is our Advocate with the Father when we miss the mark of righteousness.

> *"My little children, these things write I unto you, that ye sin not. And if any man sin, we have an advocate with the Father, Jesus Christ the righteous:" (1 John 2:1).*

The Greek word for advocate, *paraklet*
intercessor, counselor, comforter. It also mear
helper, and *standby.* These are qualities of
expressed in us as we yield ourselves to be inta
others as He is for us. As you increase your intercession,
mature in the things of God, and His attributes will increas-
ingly be expressed in and through you. The Word of God and
the Spirit of God work mightily to produce these character-
istics in you.

> *"And as we have borne the image of the*
> *earthy, we shall also bear the image of the*
> *heavenly" (1 Corinthians 15:49).*

God expects us to produce the fruit of righteousness to
His glory. As we express His image, it can only produce
godliness in our character and works.

When we intercede, we not only cause fruit to be
produced in the kingdom of God for others, we produce fruit
for ourselves as well. Everything in the Word of God is given
to us for our benefit. It is for our growth and spiritual maturity. It is to be received, not taken away.

> *"Ye have not chosen me, but I have chosen*
> *you, and ordained you, that ye should go*
> *and bring forth fruit, and that your fruit*
> *should remain: that whatsoever ye shall*
> *ask of the Father in my name, he may give*
> *it you" (John 15:16).*

Displacing Darkness

The ones who produce the fruit of righteousness are strong, dependable, and bear another's burden.

"We then that are strong ought to bear the infirmities of the weak, and not to please ourselves" (Romans 15:1).

The word *bear* in Greek, *bastaz,* means *to lift up, to bear up and away, to endure, to sustain with pre-meditated intent.* In other words, it means to completely remove the weight. In this verse, infirmities (*asthenema*) does not mean sickness or disease, but rather a scruple of conscience. It has to do with being in darkness due to being ignorant of God's Word, and thereby having a mind that is not renewed by the Word of God.

As we intercede, we bear away the darkness of the object of intercession, so that light can come in. When the light comes, people are free to make a choice for God. We don't have the power over someone's will, but we intercede and displace the forces of darkness so that the person is able to see clearly and make the right decision. Our prayer is that they will do what is right without being influenced by the spiritual forces of darkness.

Most people do not intentionally set out to make bad choices. No matter what the circumstances, they feel they are making the right choices for themselves as they see it. Of course, hindsight is better than foresight, and with the wisdom of consequences, we can recognize poor decisions. Foresight, however, is dependent on clarity and under-standing of the outcome of decisions. In prayer, we remove evil influences that blind people to seeing outcomes that may be harmful. Therefore, when the forces of darkness that ke people bound are removed, the right decisions can be maue.

The life and lifestyle of intercession is a great walk of faith that serves the kingdom of heaven. You become an expression of the love of Christ and a prayer warrior in the earth. The Lord recently revealed to me that He is raising up sacred warriors for such a time as this. Sacred warriors will be skillful in the ministry of intercessory prayer because they express the love of God.

"Greater love hath no man than this, that a man lay down his life for his friends" (John 15:13).

In First Peter 2:9, it tells us that we are a royal priest-hood. A priest is an intercessor and a bridge builder in the sense that he or she is one who brings two sides together. Jesus is the High Priest of our confession (Hebrews 3:1). Because of His sacrifice, we have direct access to the Father. When we lay our lives down in intercession, we build the bridge to Christ for the individual for whom we are inter-ceding. We become a co-laborer with Christ, bringing people into His kingdom. There is no greater love than facilitating the restoration of a lost one to God.

Build Prayer Stamina

Many people in the Body of Christ think they are not called to the ministry of intercession because they have not built up the endurance to pray an hour a day in the Spirit, much less many hours as some intercessors do. They then shy away from intercession completely. This is a very serious misperception of intercession and intercessors. While not everyone yields himself or herself to the ministry of intercession, every believer is called to be an intercessor.

Your capacity for intercession grows as your time of intercession enlarges. Stamina increases with practice. If you begin with a few minutes, don't become discouraged. Begin where you are and allow the Holy Spirit to expand your capacity for prayer. Focus on consistency and faithfulness to it. After you have developed daily consistency in your current capacity, begin to increase your prayer life and then become faithful to that. Revelation, understanding and ability to accomplish what we desire opens in the *doing* of the Word. In the *doing*, we increase in knowledge and make ourselves available for greater revelation.

Spending time in prayer can be compared to physical exercise. The apostle Paul made this analogy.

> *"For physical training is of some value (useful for a little), but godliness (spiritual training) is useful and of value in everything and in every way, for it holds promise for the present life and also for the life which is to come" (1 Timothy 4:8 AMP).*

The ability to walk in a full, enriching life of intercession is already within every born again believer. That ability needs to be exercised so that it grows to maturity. Actually, we have an obligation to do so.

God Almighty is quickening the Body of Christ to stop being "pew warmers" or like the spectators at a sporting event. We are responsible for the knowledge we have been given, *"...For unto whomsoever much is given, of him shall be much required..." (Luke 12:48).*

Begin right where you are and plan for increase. Know that by the Holy Spirit, your prayers may be going to the uttermost parts of the earth. It is quite possible that some day, not only will your prayers reach out to far away places with strange sounding names, but God may send you there to speak to them face to face, telling them of the power that is in intercession. This is the arm of intercession extended and at work. Intercession opens doors for all God given ministry.

Spiritual Code Talkers

When we pray collectively, we become united as one body. We speak and act as one, but with the strength of many. It will cause disagreements, strife, jealousy, and envy to be washed away. That is a supernatural principle. The concept of the strength of this kind of unity can even be seen in the story of the unrighteous tower of Babel.

"And the LORD said, Behold, the people is one, and they have all one language; and this they begin to do: and now nothing will be restrained from them, which they have imagined to do" (Genesis 11:6).

If the unrighteous can band together in such unity to accomplish a single goal, how much more can the Body of Christ accomplish when they become united in the spirit! When we begin to speak with one voice, one language, that of the Holy Spirit, we are unstoppable because the *"...love of God is shed abroad in our hearts by the Holy Spirit..." (Romans 5:5).*

The power of God is found in the love of God, which never fails. The more you pray in tongues, the more love is shed abroad in your heart. As a result, the more power you have flowing out from you. When you are walking in the God kind of love, it will dissolve all bitterness, resentment, and strife.

God has given us the tongues of men and of angels for the ministry of intercession. Satan knows the power of tongues, which is why he fights praying in tongues so hard. He is a fallen angel. He spoke with the tongues of angels and knows full well the power that is in and on those words. In fact, he is afraid of them.

"For he that speaketh in an unknown tongue speaketh not unto men, but unto God: for no man understandeth him; howbeit in the spirit he speaketh mysteries" (1 Corinthians 14:2).

As we speak in other tongues, we are speaking mysteries. Strong's Lexicon defines mysteries, in this verse as *"being secret or mystery (through the idea of silence imposed by initiation into religious rites)."* In other words, intercession is like a secret code. It is like the military that uses a secret code to prevent the enemy from intercepting privileged information or sabotaging top secret military assignments.

During WWII, Navajo soldiers were used to communicate secret information in the Navajo language. The enemy was unable to crack the code of the Native American language and it was highly effective in the Pacific campaign. God gave us a secret language that speaks mysteries in the spirit realm. Humans were not the first to think of a secret code. God is so wise, isn't He! When we intercede, mysteries are unfolded, revealed, and unveiled from the spirit to the mind. Then understanding of the mysteries of God begin to come.

I once ministered at an ICFCM (International Convention of Faith Churches and Ministers) conference on this very topic. During the meetings, some friends and I purposed to spend time in intercession, and eight of us met together on that Thursday evening to intercede. Instantly, the Spirit of intercession fell upon me and I had a vision in the realm of the spirit. I saw huge block letters that spelled T-U-R-K-S, and I saw a man dressed in traditional Turkish garb. I perceived that I was interceding for the Turkish people. To my knowledge, I had never interceded for them before. I began to groan and travail for the Turkish nation.

Two days later, after having ministered in the healing line, a Korean woman came up to me to greet me. She began to explain that she had a disease so close to her brain that the doctors could not operate on it. She was facing certain death unless God performed a miracle. I said to her, *"When I pray for you, not only will you speak fluently in God's heavenly language, but you are going to be healed of that disease in the Name of Jesus!"*

The Lord revealed something to me in the Spirit about that woman. I perceived that she was under a curse. The word Buddha kept coming up from my spirit. As I ministered to her, I discovered from her that her uncle had the keys to the greatest Buddhist temple in Korea in his possession. That meant that he had a high position of authority as a Buddhist religious leader. When she married an American

Christian missionary, the family spoke curses on her and her husband. This illness was the result of those curses. Nevertheless, she was healed, delivered, and set free by the power of Almighty God.

The most astonishing thing that this couple shared with me was the fact that they were missionaries who were to depart a few months later to minister to the **Turks**. I said to that precious couple, *"Go, in the Name of the Lord. You will be safe on your journey and you will be blessed. The Lord is with you. Your way has been prepared."*

I could tell them that absolute truth because of the supernatural intercession the Holy Spirit had used me in the night before. This time, intercession prepared the way for someone else. I believe many souls were saved as a result. Therefore, once again we see the effectual prayer of one member of the Body of Christ for other members. What a life of joy and well-being!

Pray With the Spirit and Understanding

"What is it then? I will pray with the spirit, and I will pray with the understanding also: I will sing with the spirit, and I will sing with the understanding also" (1 Corinthians 14:15).

There are two things that the Spirit of the Lord shared with me concerning praying with understanding. The first is to know the need of the individual for whom you are praying. The second is to apply the specific Word of God to the particular desire or need, that is, find the scripture that fits the need and stand on it as the basis for your petition. Obviously, this would be praying with our understanding in our known language.

Praying with the Spirit is praying in tongues. You can do this any time and any where. The only place I find it hard to do this is when I am brushing my teeth. Paul, speaking by the Holy Spirit, puts praying in the Spirit as being first. It speaks of Paul's priority and understanding of the workings of the spiritual world.

The Word of God is like a seed. When it is planted into the soul of a person, it must be watered by meditation on it and by prayer. As it is watered, it begins to grow. It is like an embryo that grows inside a womb for nine months, and then in the fullness of time, the child is delivered. Similarly, the seed of the Word of God, either planted through the reading of the written Word, or the spoken Word through preaching or prophesying, is planted into a person's heart.

> *"Being born again, not of corruptible seed, but of incorruptible, by the word of God, which liveth and abideth for ever" (1 Peter 1:23).*

The ministry of intercessory prayer fertilizes that Word and continues to do so until it reaches full maturity. When the seed of the Word reaches full maturity, travail (earnest prayer) begins to take place. There is never spiritual birth without travail, and birth is inevitable.

> *"My little children, of whom I travail in birth again until Christ be formed in you," (Galatians 4:19).*

We are one in Christ Jesus, for "...*he that is joined unto the Lord is one Spirit" (1 Corinthians 6:17).* We are bone of His bone and flesh of His flesh. You may be doing just fine yourself, but a brother or sister in China or elsewhere may be experiencing torture for their faith. You may suddenly feel that burden come upon you, feeling anguish in your heart. It is the Spirit of intercession coming upon you. God is calling for your reinforcement in prayer to help lift the burden off someone, so that they can have the grace they need to sustain themselves in their time of need.

After I finished teaching on this one afternoon, a pastor approached me to discuss an experience he had. He said that there had been a season of time in prayer when every time he went into intercession; he would see a woman's breasts. This really disturbed him for some time because he thought that he must be dealing with lust in his own heart. However, that was not the case. His wife was later diagnosed with breast cancer and had to have both breasts removed. In his prayer life, he was receiving a word of knowledge. God was actually trying to alert him to pray for his wife, but he didn't realize this until she went through this trauma.

Whenever you are feeling just great and then suddenly it seems as if you are stricken down with depression or worry not really knowing why, it is that Spirit of intercession falling on you. You don't have to be in church for this to happen. It might even be at the checkout line at the grocery store. It is your clue to spend time in intercession on behalf of a serious need for someone.

> "*...pray one for another, that ye may be healed. The effectual fervent prayer of a righteous man availeth much" (James 5:16).*

Repairers of the Breach

Repairers of the Breach

"Continue in prayer, and watch in the same with thanksgiving;

Withal praying also for us, that God would open unto us a door of utterance, to speak the mystery of Christ, for which I am also in bonds:

That I may make it manifest, as I ought to speak" (Colossians 4:2-4).

In 1979, the Lord revealed to me that He would send me forth specifically to teach His people about intercessory prayer. He opened great doors of opportunity for me both in the United States and abroad. I ministered in Jamaica and for one month in Israel, where I saw phenomenal things take place. Since then, He has expanded my ministry both in scope and distance. All of it began and continues to be anchored in prayer.

For one year during 1980, I taught on the ministry of intercessory prayer everywhere the Lord sent me. I taught by precept and practice (teach and do) as the Lord instructed me. For some time that year, I felt like I was plowing my way through dense foliage with a machete. Even though there were those very eager to enter into a lifestyle of committed prayer, there were others who didn't appreciate the idea that you need to do something for someone else. Nevertheless, I cut through, planted the seeds, and the Lord had the victory. It is wonderful to revisit those places that were formerly some hard ground and now have become an open heaven.

Revival

There are seasons of an open heaven for the Body of Christ at large and we call them revivals because new life is breathed upon that which needs change. Revivals like the recent Brownsville and Toronto revivals, much like those in the past, come in waves. These spiritual outpourings bring about repentance and miracles. People are born again; backsliders return to Christ; and people experience the blessings of the Holy Spirit.

Whereas each one seems to bring a special focus, they are all invariably launched and sustained through prayer. The magnitude of what intercessors bring forth in prayer for revival may not even be revealed to them until it manifests, but when it comes, the entire Body of Christ is blessed.

Fanner Bees

Many times God uses nature to teach us about the ways of the Spirit. A few years ago, the Lord gave me insight about intercession through understanding fanner bees. This type of bee stays at the entrance of the hive. They beat their little wings very fast and create what is called a "fray mist." That is their work. It is what they are designed to do. As they do this, it creates a wind tunnel in the hive, pulling in good air and pushing the bad air out. As intercessors, we pull in the good air, the wind of the Holy Spirit, and push out the bad air of flesh and darkness. When there is a congregation of believers coming together in one mind and in one accord to work like the fanner bees clearing the atmosphere, the effects are supernatural.

While ministering in Seoul, Korea, I found that the ministry of intercession is so strong that the church had to ring a bell to let the thousands of people know to stop praying. They prayed with such fervor and earnestness that the atmosphere was supercharged with the energy of Almighty God. That type of praying is beyond the natural. It pushes the veil of flesh out and gets one into the supernatural place of His glory. This Korean church has over a million believers, but the magnitude of growth it experienced could not have happened without their fervent prayer.

Become His Workmanship

For us to have the supernatural working in and through us, we must yield to the Holy Spirit. He does not violate our free will. He will not flow through us any more than we allow. We must be focused on Almighty God with no room for ego, self aggrandizement, or even public embarrassment about intercession. You have to come to the place in your walk with the Lord that you just don't care what anyone thinks. Determine that you are His, you belong to Him, and he is creating good workmanship. That includes chiseling, burning, and stripping away a lot of everything that is not godly in our lives, but in the end, the workmanship is superb. It is Jesus working in us for His good pleasure.

I was in a service in Norway where there was such freshness and newness for the release of the Holy Spirit in a powerful way. I came to the pulpit to speak and when I opened my mouth, I prophesied the Word of the Lord. Speaking of intercession, I said something like, *"What will you do with what I am doing? What will you do with My agenda?"* God was issuing forth a sober call to pray. His agenda is in the ever present "now" and we continually seek to complete it.

I believe that prayer is challenged more than any other church activity. It is really not surprising because the devil knows the power that has been given to us, and that his dominion of darkness is defeated when we pray. Because there is direct communication with God in prayer, he is not invited to participate and intercession swallows up the darkness. It is something we choose to do out of God's love in us, and that love casts out all fear.

Prayer is not a method or a formula. It is not something that we have to do as a religious ritual out of compulsion or because it makes us appear holy. People really cannot be forced to pray. Repetitious murmuring without heartfelt communication with God is nothing more than empty words. It bears no fruit in the believer's life, and neither does it do anything for the situation or need for which they are praying.

"But when ye pray, use not vain repetitions, as the heathen do: for they think that they shall be heard for their much speaking" (Matthew 6:7).

Prayer is simply an outflow of the in-working of the Holy Spirit. There has to be a willingness to yield to it.

Make Time for Prayer

Over the years, I have discovered that prayer is easier when we set aside a divine appointment with God to pray. Just say to yourself, *"This is my time with the Lord."* Like setting time aside for meals, it becomes habitual. In fact, when you miss a meal, it disrupts your routine and your body lets you know something is missing.

Prayer life is much the same. Your capacity for prayer is equal to your determination, purpose, and quality of prayer. We grow in prayer, and prayer grows with us. The more you pray, the more you will want to pray. It becomes habitual, and it becomes like an addiction, only it's a good one. That is exactly what a habit is, an addiction to a particular action. We begin to crave and long for times spent in communion with God.

We really need to have habits in the realm of the spirit because this is where we mature. A healthy enriched prayer life happens when you determine to make it happen by routinely setting aside that special time with God. In our busy lives we may think we have no time for prayer, yet we always find time for what we believe is important. If life or death hinged on taking time for prayer, we would certainly find the time, but ironically, our spiritual lives really do depend on it.

Even when we keep our appointments of prayer with God, the enemy tempts you to feel as if we are not accomplishing anything. By the direction of the Holy Spirit, I went on a forty day time of fasting and prayer. During that time, I really had to fight disappointment because I did not sense that it was accomplishing a great deal. However, it was after I came off the fast that I began to see the power of God manifest. The greatest work that the Lord had done during those forty days was done in my heart. That is where it counted most. If we are to be all that He desires, then we must submit ourselves to Him and allow the Spirit to work His will into and through us.

I imagine that it must be exciting to God when He knows we are going to have time with Him. I can visualize God having a "spiritual watch," and He would be looking at it, excited that we are coming at the appointed time to visit with Him. We should be equally excited to have time with Him.

David set appointed times for prayer and he was known to be a man after God's heart. Throughout the Bible there are God's men and women who were powerful people of prayer who knew to keep their appointments with God. Every biblical hero or heroine (Esther, Moses, Joshua, Mary, Paul, the prophets, just to name a few) spent time in prayer and knew the voice of God. There would be no other way they could have had success. They learned the voice of God in their times of communion with Him and they were willing to be obedient to His voice.

In Luke 6, we find that Jesus spent all night with the Father, and afterward appointed twelve disciples by the leading of the Spirit.

> *"And it came to pass in those days, that he went out into a mountain to pray, and continued all night in prayer to God.*
>
> *And when it was day, he called unto him his disciples: and of them he chose twelve, whom also he named apostles" (Luke 6:12,13).*

He received revelation in the prayer closet. The same truth will work for those who pray today. Revelation comes during prayer.

As we noted earlier, eighteenth century revivalist Jonathan G. Edwards said, *"When God has something very great to accomplish for His church, it is His will that there should precede it the extraordinary prayers of His people. And it is revealed that when God is about to accomplish great things for His church, He will begin by remarkably pouring out the Spirit of grace and supplication."* We are not left alone to pray, driven by our own commitment or dedication. It comes to us as God pours out His Spirit of grace and supplication.

*"And I will pour upon the house of David,
and upon the inhabitants of Jerusalem,
the spirit of grace and of supplications:
and they shall look upon me whom they
have pierced, and they shall mourn for
him, as one mourneth for his only son, and
shall be in bitterness for him, as one that
is in bitterness for his firstborn"
(Zechariah 12:10).*

During times of prayer, reality comes into focus. The
Spirit of the Lord causes the people you are interceding for
to be able to perceive the way things really are. They begin
to understand why things happen the way they do and how
things should be according to the will of God. Once that
happens they cry out to God. That is revival. The things of
the Spirit are eternal, steadfast, and reliable.

*"Jesus Christ the same yesterday, and to
day, and for ever" (Hebrews 13:8).*

There was once a time in my life when I no longer
wanted to teach on intercession even though I continued
intercession in my personal prayer life. For a season, the
magnitude of teaching on intercession actually did stop
because of abuses and criticisms that floated about when
people did not understand what they were doing. They were
operating in the flesh and called it intercession, and then
legitimate intercessors were swept with the same brush as
being weird. You see, the devil hates intercession and he will
stop at nothing to quench it right out of the Body of Christ.
Nevertheless, the devil cannot stop the real thing and now,
more than ever, intercession is coming to the forefront. The
Body of Christ is learning to discern the difference between
real intercession and that which is flesh.

Wheel of Birth

ιe tongue is a fire. [The tongue is a] of wickedness set among our ʹs, contaminating and depraving ιne whole body and setting on fire the wheel of birth (the cycle of man's nature), being itself ignited by hell (Gehenna)" (James 3:6 AMP).

The tongue is the instrument of expression, and in intercession it is what makes it turn. That is what brings the things of the Spirit into manifestation in the natural. It works both negatively and positively. The tongue can be set on fire of hell or by the Holy Spirit. Either way, what you speak will come into existence.

In a positive way, the tongue is set on fire by the Holy Spirit and then the "wheel of birth" toward the things that the Father desires comes to pass in our lives. In 1997, the Lord told me, *"People do not change by control or manipulation. It takes the breath of the Holy Spirit breathing life over and into them before they can change."* I have tried to change people, but was never successful. I only got a lot of stress, anxiety, and frustration, but not a smidgen of results. The only thing that works is the penetrating power of the Word of God by the Holy Spirit. Then the Lord added, *"Therefore, **turn** your talk to prayer."*

My deepest desire is for people to acquire the habit of prayer. When we do that we will come to understand the power of agreement as we have never before known it in our generation. What we speak will come to pass, right or wrong, negative or positive, so let's agree on good things. Good things will then surely come to pass.

Test the Spirits

There is danger in ministering to God's people without spending time alone with the Lord. There have been ministers who have privately told me something like, *"I flowed in the Spirit of God and I worked in the word of knowledge. However, I stepped beyond the line of the work of the Holy Spirit and began to operate in that gift on my own. It opened the door to familiar spirits."* This can happen when we don't serve Him rightly and don't treat his gifts and callings as holy. The source is cut off.

Someone can say, *"Well, it worked before,"* and keep right on using the giftings without spending time with God in His presence. The supply of grace and power runs out, and in its place are the workings of demonic familiar spirits. That is where they get into trouble.

They appear to be working in spiritual giftings. You may ask, *"How can that person know so much about me and my situation if it is not the work of God being done through them?"* It may look right, but they can be giving heed to *familiar* spirits, who are *familiar* with you. This was the case of Balaam (Numbers 22-24). He was truly a prophet, but because he merchandised his anointing, he was tempted to curse Israel. Had Balaam stayed close to God, he would not have used his spiritual gifts to serve the purpose of darkness.

How can you know the difference? You must become a person acquainted with the ways of the Holy Spirit yourself in order to know. That means that you must become a person of prayer in order to discern such things. Your spirit will bear witness with the Holy Spirit and will never violate the Word of God when it is right. It is not the Lord's desire that we be ignorant.

"Beloved, believe not every spirit, but try the spirits whether they are of God: because many false prophets are gone out into the world.

Hereby know ye the Spirit of God: Every spirit that confesseth that Jesus Christ is come in the flesh is of God:" (1 John 4:1,2).

You see, people can minister very successfully while not living righteously, but God cannot honor the anointing without character. When ministers are not living righteously, they still have gifts operating. As Romans 11:29 says, *"For the gifts and calling of God are without repentance."* This means that gifts and callings of God on people's lives are not revoked when they are not serving Him. Gifts cannot be earned. Nevertheless, even though God is long-suffering, he does not tolerate unrighteous and unrepentant behavior endlessly. In addition, when people are not living right before God, they open themselves up to evil influence and destruction. As First John says, we must try the spirits to make sure they are of God and we must keep ourselves close to God in prayer and in His Word so that we can clearly know His voice.

When we don't balance our lives with prayer and study of the Word of God, all sorts of weird ideas and behaviors infiltrate the church. Because of abuses and lack of godly wisdom, intercessors have unfairly been targeted with a reputation that brings raised eyebrows and downward glances. Sadly, many people paint all intercessors with the same brush when things go wrong. Nevertheless, I have never known of a <u>praying</u> pastor who was afraid of a few intercessors that were a bit "unusual." An anointed and ordained pastor is not intimidated by true Holy Spirit inspired intercessory prayer, which may at times seem strange, nor the process of helping people grow into such a ministry, though there be mistakes made along the way. God gives divine wisdom in how to make corrections to bring this viable ministry of intercession into divine order and stability.

Hindrances to Prayer

Many years ago I asked the Lord how strong intercessors who are led by the Holy Spirit can become "flaky." The Lord showed me that the intercessor who does not develop godly character, walking in the Spirit and bearing the fruit of the Spirit, opens doors to the work of the flesh. Obedience to God's Word is always the safe territory. This, of course, implies that people spend time getting to know the Word of God. Doing so gives no place to the devil or flesh.

The Word of God gives very specific directives about hindrances to prayer. One of the tremendous hindrances is unforgiveness.

Jesus spoke on this very issue when He preached the Sermon on the Mount of Beatitudes. He operated in pure love and expects us to do the same. This clears the path for love to never fail.

> *"Therefore if thou bring thy gift to the altar, and there rememberest that thy brother hath ought against thee;*
>
> *Leave there thy gift before the altar, and go thy way; first be reconciled to thy brother, and then come and offer thy gift"* *(Matthew 5:23,24).*

When you enter into prayer, check your heart to make sure you are free from the encumbrances of bearing grudges, or holding on to hurts. Forgive those who have wronged you so that you can enter into the liberty of prayer.

Doubt and unbelief is another hindrance to successful prayer. How can we expect to receive from God if we don't believe that He will fulfill His promises? His Word is rich with precious promises for every human situation, and it is His desire to bless us with them.

> *"But let him ask in faith, nothing wavering. For he that wavereth is like a wave of the sea driven with the wind and tossed.*
>
> *For let not that man think that he shall receive any thing of the Lord" (James 1:6-7).*
>
> *"But without faith it is impossible to please him: for he that cometh to God must believe that he is, and that he is a rewarder of them that diligently seek him" (Hebrews 11:6).*

Lastly, flagrant sin is another hindrance to prayer. The guilt of unrepentant sin is a sure stopper that plugs up even the desire to pray. Psalm 66:18 says, *"If I regard iniquity in my heart, the Lord will not hear me."* The remedy is so simple. It only requires a humble heart to confess the sin and receive God's forgiveness.

> *"If we confess our sins, he is faithful and just to forgive us our sins, and to cleanse us from all unrighteousness" (1 John 1:9).*

It is God's desire that we are fruitful in answered prayer.

"If ye abide in me, and my words abide in you, ye shall ask what ye will, and it shall be done unto you.

Herein is my Father glorified, that ye bear much fruit; so shall ye be my disciples" *(John 15:7,8).*

Hindrances stop the flow of that fruitfulness, but these hindrances do not have to be a permanent condition. Forgiving others who have wronged you; repenting of sin and receiving God's forgiveness; and believing His Word for every situation are essential not only for your own spiritual health, but to keeping your heart in a ready state to intercede on behalf of others.

Holy and Royal

We know that it is God's desire for us to *"...walk worthy of the Lord unto all pleasing, being fruitful in every good work, and increasing in the knowledge of God;"* **(Colossians 1:10),** yet in our imperfect human condition, repeatedly needing cleansing from failures, how are we to walk worthy? In our own natural state, it is impossible. That is what Jesus accomplished for us. He is our righteousness, and because He ever lives to be the bridge between God and humanity, He in us and we in Him, makes us worthy.

He is the ultimate High Priest and King of Righteousness.

In the Old Testament, it was impossible for an Israelite to be a priest and king at the same time. Priests were of the tribe of Levi, who did not have an inheritance of land because they were separated unto their work as priests.

They were supported financially by the rest of the tribes. Kings came out of the tribe of Judah, particularly from the lineage of David.

There is, however, a remarkable person in Abraham's lifetime that stands out and defies this rule. Melchizedek, meaning king of righteousness, was king of Salem, meaning king of peace. Just in those two names, we see a prophetic model of the One Who fulfilled the Law and became priest and king, Jesus Christ.

> *"The LORD hath sworn, and will not repent, Thou art a priest for ever after the order of Melchizedek" (Psalm 110:4).*

Abraham submitted to Melchizedek and gave him a tenth of all that he owned, which became the precedence for the tithe, and Abraham was blessed by Melchizedek.

Hebrews 7 tells us even more about Melchizedek, and describes him as a great man, worthy of receiving Abraham's offering, who has no stated origins and was made like the Son of God, a priest forever (Hebrews 7:3, 4). Further on we learn that Jesus, born of the kingly tribe of Judah, is made a priest not by law (Levitical priesthood), but according to the power of indestructible life (Hebrews 7:16). Jesus is the High Priest and King after the order of Melchizedek forever because He lives forever. That is why He is able to continuously provide salvation. He ever lives to make intercession. He is the mediator of a better covenant as Hebrews 8:6 states.

Levitical priests needed to make daily sacrifices for their own sins first, and then for the sins of others. Jesus, Who is *"...holy, harmless, undefiled, separate from sinners, and made higher than the heavens;"* (Hebrews 7:26), has no need of the daily rituals. He is the sacrificed lamb, Whose blood continuously cleanses His people from all unrighteousness. This is why we are worthy and holy. We can approach God cleansed by the pure blood of Jesus, and we can present our intercession with confidence as a holy people who are priests and kings with Jesus.

> *"But ye are a chosen generation, a royal priesthood, an holy nation, a peculiar people; that ye should shew forth the praises of him who hath called you out of darkness into his marvellous light;" (1 Peter 2:9).*

God has declared our servanthood, our priesthood, and kingship.

> *"Ye also, as lively stones, are built up a spiritual house, an holy priesthood, to offer up spiritual sacrifices, acceptable to God by Jesus Christ" (1 Peter 2:5).*

In the role of holy priest, we bring the sacrifice of praise and worship, waiting on Him. Intercession is always preceded by praise and worship, acknowledging His dominion and authority over all things, and expressing love for Him. That is sweet incense that rises up before the Lord. That is where we learn to obey Him. We learn to hear Him in the quiet times spent in His presence, hearing His voice, knowing His heart's desire and pleasure. This releases desire and motivation within us to be a willing and obedient holy person in Christ.

From praise and worship, we move into intercession. It is motivated by love that proceeds from the time spent with the Father. God is perfect love. It is impossible to have been in His presence and not be changed by that love, and to be molded more into His image. His glory changes us. We begin to love others because we love God. It all flows from the same fountain, the same source. It gives us all the strength and resources that we need to be the royal priests and holy nation.

Our Redeemer lives in us, and the Holy Spirit manifests His redemption through us. We can be the priests of God in the earth, to stand between needy people and God Almighty. There has been enough gossip and faultfinding in the Body of Christ, which grieves the heart of the Father. Through intercession we can be used as instruments of grace in eliminating these sins.

> *"And they that shall be of thee shall build the old waste places: thou shalt raise up the foundations of many generations; and thou shalt be called, The repairer of the breach, The restorer of paths to dwell in"* *(Isaiah 58:12).*

The more we begin to comprehend this, the more we walk in its truth. Jesus is the High Priest. He literally became bridge builder, the repairer of the chasm between God and humanity. Every time we come to the Father in the Name of Jesus, we cross that bridge to God. He repaired the breach between man and God with His own blood sacrifice and restored the path leading home. As priests unto God, we build a bridge of prayer that will enable broken people to touch the face of God.

> *"Wherefore he is able also to save them to the uttermost that come unto God by him, seeing he ever liveth to make intercession for them"* *(Hebrews 7:25).*

Through the power of intercessory prayer and the work of Christ in us, we restore the paths. We walk as He walked on the earth and live as He ever lives today.

Make Up the Hedge

"And I sought for a man among them, that should make up the hedge, and stand in the gap before me for the land, that I should not destroy it: but I found none" (Ezekiel 22:30).

The word *hedge* (*gader* in Hebrew) means an enclosure, wall or fence. Gardeners plant hedges to establish borders around properties or protective boundaries around a garden. Intercession sets up a wall of protection.

When a disaster suddenly overtakes an individual, there is a gap in the protective elements in their life. It could be a weakness, a failure, a sin, an attack of the enemy in a place that is not strong. Because the individual has a hole in their "hedge" their life is open to the enemy. They don't have the strength to protect themselves from the adversary's attack. The intercessor stands in the gap, filling the opening in the wall of their lives. We become like a fortress in the midst of the battle until they can recover or repent and no longer have the hole in the hedge.

How does God see the hedge? He is holy and righteous. He desires for His people to walk in His protection, yet He remembers our frame and that we are dust. He has given us the ministry of intercession so that He can help in the time of need. We work together with Him to shore up the weaknesses of humanity. As we intercede, standing in the hole in the walls of people's lives, we cover the hole that would allow the enemy to damage their lives. This intercessory position allows God to work in them, giving them the opportunity to choose His way and recover themselves from Satan's strongholds and works of the flesh. Once they choose God, they have no hole in their wall. What a privilege!

Intercession is love in action. Love not only covers a multitude of sins, love prevents a multitude of sins. Becoming a priest of intercession unto Almighty God means you are standing in faith in the gap and praying for as long as it takes for God to work His will through others until He can deposit something into them that will make their hedge strong. They are complete when the gap is filled.

Paul's apostolic prayers and declarations of blessings are laced throughout the epistles indicating that Paul regularly prayed for the Body of Christ to grow in spiritual revelation. He recognized that prayer is an essential ministry to the Body of Christ so that as the Body of Christ grows in wisdom and revelation of Him, they become strong, fully encompassed by God's blessings and protection. Two examples are in the letters to the Ephesians and Colossians.

> *"Wherefore I also, after I heard of your faith in the Lord Jesus, and love unto all the saints,*
>
> *Cease not to give thanks for you, making mention of you in my prayers;*
>
> *That the God of our Lord Jesus Christ, the Father of glory, may give unto you the spirit of wisdom and revelation in the knowledge of him:*
>
> *The eyes of your understanding being enlightened; that ye may know what is the hope of his calling, and what the riches of the glory of his inheritance in the saints,*
>
> *And what is the exceeding greatness of his power to us-ward who believe, according to the working of his mighty power"* *(Ephesians 1:15-19).*

"For this cause we also, since the day we heard it, do not cease to pray for you, and to desire that ye might be filled with the knowledge of his will in all wisdom and spiritual understanding;

That ye might walk worthy of the Lord unto all pleasing, being fruitful in every good work, and increasing in the knowledge of God;

Strengthened with all might, according to his glorious power, unto all patience and longsuffering with joyfulness;

Giving thanks unto the Father, which hath made us meet to be partakers of the inheritance of the saints in light:

Who hath delivered us from the power of darkness, and hath translated us into the kingdom of his dear Son:

In whom we have redemption through his blood, even the forgiveness of sins" (Colossians 1:9-14).

It was Paul's ministry to equip the Body of Christ and prayer is part of that equipping. We can pray these prayers over the Body of Christ today because these words inspired by the Holy Spirit are eternal.

Ministry of Intercessory Prayer

We think of ministers as apostles, prophets, evangelists, pastors, and teachers. They are indeed ministers, but these are their functions in the church. It describes their responsibilities and the specific plan that God has for them. The word minister is simply one who serves. Ministers are people who God calls to serve the Body of Christ. In that sense, all believers have a ministry. Some minister in helps, some minister in administration, some have specific groups to whom they minister, as in nurseries. The list of places to serve the church can be very long.

Intercessory prayer is also a ministry. In fact it is a "front line" ministry that goes before to pave the way for other ministries. Intercession serves all of humanity because prayer goes forth for the saved, the unsaved, the hurt, the vision of the church, and so on.

Intercessory prayer is a calling to individuals, and all in the Body are called to intercede. However, we find that there are individuals who yield themselves more deeply and frequently to intercession, and as they increase their intercession, they receive more grace for it. They don't mind being awakened in the middle of the night to get up and pray for a pressing need. They seem to thrive on interceding for the needs of others. In this sense, they are called as ministers of intercession, but it is not an exclusive club. All are welcome and encouraged to give their lives to intercession.

Pray Without Ceasing

"And said unto them, It is written, My house shall be called the house of prayer; but ye have made it a den of thieves" (Matthew 21:13).

Jesus said these words as He was cleansing the Temple of the moneychangers, who were profiting from the requirements of Jews to attend the services of the high holy days. The Temple had is own currency, different from that of the Roman government that was ruling Judea, and so people had to exchange government currency for temple currency in order to purchase the animals for sacrifice. They came from far distances and were really at the mercy of the moneychangers, who abused their position and charged exorbitant fees, making the temple, God's house of prayer, a den of thieves. They merchandised the things of God and it angered Jesus with a holy anger.

The Lord revealed to me that when we do not avail ourselves and obey the call of prayer, we become as robbers and thieves. We rob God, ourselves, and others of God's power to affect the lives of people.

Another place where holy anger is expressed is where the prophet Samuel became very upset with the Israelites when they insisted on having a king. Up to that time, it was God's direction in giving them judges to rule, but since they demanded a king, they got Saul, which did not turn out to be good for them. Samuel must have been very frustrated because he could not convince them differently. Nevertheless, he urged them to stay faithful to the Lord.

"And Samuel said unto the people, Fear not: ye have done all this wickedness: yet turn not aside from following the LORD, but serve the LORD with all your heart;

And turn ye not aside: for then should ye go after vain things, which cannot profit nor deliver; for they are vain.

For the LORD will not forsake his people for his great name's sake: because it hath pleased the LORD to make you his people.

Moreover as for me, God forbid that I should sin against the LORD in ceasing to

*pray for you: but I will teach you the good
and the right way:" (1 Samuel 12:20-23).*

In spite of their demands to go against God's ways, Samuel committed himself to pray for them and teach them what is right. Ultimately, Samuel obediently followed God's directions, found God's choice, and anointed David to be king. Samuel was a praying man and his endurance brought him to God's perfect will.

This revelation became very clear to me as I was praying for a certain individual. It was a long time of intercession and I reached my saturation point. I just did not care any more. It just did not matter to me as I had lost the right kind of care. Suddenly, one day the Lord corrected me saying, *"Don't give up on that person, don't let them go."* Sometimes, you and I are the only people who stand between an individual and hell. We stand between them and the works of darkness. Let us pray without ceasing on their behalf.

Perhaps the Lord allows us to get to that saturation point in intercession so that we cast all of our cares upon Him. We get out of the way so that He can get in the way to deal with the situation. We just need to pray.

> *"And let us not be weary in well doing: for
> in due season we shall reap, if we faint
> not" (Galatians 6:9).*

Resistance Builds Strength

As we pray, we sometimes encounter resistance. When we are not strong enough, the resistance can negate what we are doing. Isaiah 44:12 tells us, *"...he is hungry, and his strength faileth: he drinketh no water, and is faint.*" In other words, when we do not eat or drink, we become weakened and faint. Our spiritual ability for resistance is built by taking in the Word of God and drinking in the Holy Spirit from the well of living water. We must daily receive the fresh bread of God's Word from heaven. The milk and the meat of the Word of God make us strong in Him and in the power of His might. The Holy Spirit infuses us with stamina to do His work.

In our weakness, His strength operates through us. Strength comes as a result of resistance. The more pressure that is put on muscle, the more it develops power and strength. The end result of praying through the storm and crisis is that greater strength comes by the Holy Spirit. A natural example is the diamond, which is formed by extreme pressure on carbon. The most precious jewel formed from common coal.

Pressure brings an end to all pretenses. The real you is exposed and then you react. The final reality is that the only way to escape the world's pressure is to go to heaven. If you are only looking to escape the pressures, you will not be of much use to the Body of Christ or the building of God's kingdom. Strength and power comes as a result of resistance in the Spirit to pressures of darkness. Staying in the Word of God and praying in the Spirit keeps us from becoming weary and fainting and we build strength.

You Are Not Your Own

These are such exciting times in the Lord. The Holy Spirit is emphasizing prayer and we see teachings in every multi media available – books, CDs, television programs, conferences. It is absolutely awesome!

There is no doubt that God is calling attention to His house of prayer. He did not call His house a house of healing, or house of deliverance, nor His house of teaching. He said that His house is a house of prayer for all people.

> *"Even them will I bring to my holy mountain, and make them joyful in my house of prayer: their burnt offerings and their sacrifices shall be accepted upon mine altar; for mine house shall be called an house of prayer for all people" (Isaiah 56:7).*

As New Covenant believers, we are the temple of God, His house of prayer. Our churches are places of worship and prayer certainly takes place there, but God inhabits temples made of flesh and blood, not brick and mortar. We no longer belong to ourselves. We have been purchased by the Blood of Jesus.

> *"What? know ye not that your body is the temple of the Holy Ghost which is in you, which ye have of God, and ye are not your own?" (1 Corinthians 3:16).*

It is in His anointing that we are even able to stand in the face of obstacles with the strength of Almighty God and see the victory. The anointing, the supernatural ability to stand and persevere to see blind eyes open, deaf ears hear, and the lame rise and walk, only comes to those who engage in fervent prayer.

Figure Eight and Blackbirds

In each of our lives, there are defining moments that are emblazoned into our memories and serve as guiding life lessons or in some cases, divine appointments with divine revelation. I had such a defining moment in April, 1983, where I ministered at a conference in California. It was at a convention center in Los Angeles one block away from Azusa Street of Pentecostal history fame. Two of the most honored leaders of intercessory prayer were there, Phil Halverson and Rachel Teafatiller. For me, they represented the generation that came before me and planted spiritual seeds that produced fruit we are still harvesting.

I was the last scheduled speaker of the conference on Saturday evening. During the entire conference, the Spirit of Lord was moving mightily and Saturday was no exception. When it came time for me to minister, I walked up to the pulpit. I held on to it with both hands to keep from falling under the glorious power of God that filled that place. It appeared to me that a thick haze settled upon the people. The glory of God had filled the room.

As I stood there, I felt someone at my right side. I looked and found Phil Halverson who had grabbed hold of my right arm. Then to my left, Rachel Teafatiller took hold of my left arm. They had come forward to uphold me because the glory of the Lord was so strong I could hardly stand. Without warning, all three of us fell flat on our backs under the power of God. No one caught us because it happened so quickly. The glory of God covered us and we laid there in His presence.

My eyes were closed and the Lord gave me a glorious vision. It was like I was taken back in time to Genesis 15 where Abram received the promise of a son in his old age and that his descendants would be numerous as the stars. Abram then was directed to bring several animals, cut them in two and lay the parts opposite each other. It was a blood sacrifice and I watched as God passed between the pieces of the offering, making it a blood covenant between God and

Abram. The path I saw was God moving through the blood sacrifice in what appeared to be a figure eight.

Eight is the number of glory, the number of resurrection and new beginnings. God was letting Abram know that something new was going to take place in his life. Something glorious was about to be released in the earth. God was giving Abram a new beginning, and for his sons and daughters after him.

After I had seen this in the Spirit, I saw something else begin to take place. I saw blackbirds swooping down over the blood sacrifice attempting to steal it away. As I watched Abram fighting off the blackbirds from the carcasses, the Spirit of the Lord spoke to me saying, "The blackbirds are coming to steal what has happened in this great intercessors conference. They will come and try to steal intercession as well as intercessors from My church. If they are not fought off, they will succeed."

From this startling vision, I understood that like Abram's promise and gift from God, the church was given a powerful revelation of intercession delivered by His servants. Many would be blessed for generations to come, just like Abram's seed were blessed through him for generations. However, Abram's seed through the generations suffered and many tried to wipe them out completely.

The blackbirds represented the evil forces that attack the Word of God and try to keep it from taking hold in believers. If the enemy could steal the promises of God, then His people cannot be blessed and they face destruction.

It didn't take very long for the blackbirds to come against the teachings and practice of intercessory prayer. As time passed and the battle against intercessory prayer became intense, I found myself shying away from teaching on it. I became silenced. I decided, "Don't even mention intercession to me again. I don't want anything more to do with it. I will pray in my prayer closet, that's it. I will not be labeled a flake."

I suppose in retrospect, I just could not stand the thought of enduring any more persecution for the sake of teaching on intercession. I felt I had to do what was more acceptable and "politically correct" in the church. I was not seeing myself through the eyes of God, but rather through the eyes of man. I was bound by a man-pleasing spirit as well as a great deal of pride. I was wrong, and apparently I was not alone in my decision to be silenced.

The blackbirds had moved into the Body of Christ just as He showed me in my vision. The words of His Spirit still echo in my heart today. Since that conference in 1983, I have witnessed the reality of it. There were not enough laborers to ward off the blackbirds.

Consequently, for a season of time, they devoured intercessors as well as intercessory prayer from God's people. The blackbirds came in through apathy, inconsistency, the need for "respectability" also known as pride, and just plain weirdness that counterfeited the world of the Spirit. The intercessors began to slip farther away from their prayer life and from His presence. Intercession became either such a familiar term that it lost its meaning, or it became an object of scorn and contempt. When this happened, the very lifeline of revival was choked.

As time came and went, I found myself once again on my face before the Lord in intercession concerning the vision of the blackbirds. It seemed as if it were seared into my spirit with a hot iron. I realized that I would no longer be able to escape or evade this issue before the Lord. It involved a year of fasting, prayer, and weeping before the Throne of God until the release came.

My flesh did not want to see or understand the things that were revealed to me during this season of fasting and prayer. The Lord showed me another vision and made me look at it. I saw that I had laid down the mantle of teaching intercession that He had placed upon my life. It was just lying there on the ground. I watched as people were tearing fragments from that beautiful mantle. I knew instantly that this meant they were taking fragmented pieces of intercession to themselves and running away with it.

The mantle in its wholeness possessed the complete prophetic intercessor's call, gifting, anointing, wisdom, knowledge, and understanding. Because the teaching of intercession had been lacking, I saw the enormous potential for misuse, confusion, and chaos. Knowledge and understanding of the ministry of intercession was incomplete and fragmented. Unfortunately, I had contributed to its incompleteness through my silence. I let what was entrusted to me by His Holy Spirit slip from me. This, I had come to know, was sin. I repented!

"Therefore we ought to give the more earnest heed to the things which we have heard, lest at any time we should let them slip" (Hebrews 2:1).

Let me add that I realize I am not the only one that carries the mantle of intercessory prayer. What I am saying is that for my portion, the decision I had made affected not only my own life, but the lives of the people to whom the Lord sent me. The very heartbeat of the ministry He had called me to was hanging in the balance and suffered.

Now that we are in a new millennium and that season has passed, many are anxiously awaiting the return of the fullness of God and what He intends for the church here and abroad. I am seeing this restoration take place in the

renewed desire to intercede and learn more about intercession. God has restored all to me and I am obedient to His
directions and leadings as He sends me forth.

At the risk of sounding redundant, I must emphasize
that we do not belong to ourselves. As intercessors, we all
have our part to play in a much larger picture than what
surrounds us in our own lives as individuals. The decisions
we make today concerning the revelations given to us by
Almighty God can profoundly affect the lives of countless
people. Of that I am sure. Do not allow the pressure from
the enemy to move you out of your gift, call, anointing, life,
and ministry.

> *"Be not afraid of their faces: for I am with
> thee to deliver thee, saith the LORD" (Jere-
> miah 1:8).*

Encouragement and Comfort

Your mantle is your life as you walk in what God
plans and purposes. He has a definitive plan for you that
will bring you total fulfillment as well bring blessings to the
Body of Christ. You alone can fulfill that which God has
designed for you.

> *"For I know the thoughts and plans that I
> have for you, says the Lord, thoughts and
> plans for welfare and peace and not for
> evil, to give you hope in your final
> outcome" (Jeremiah 29:11 AMP).*

Your mantle is your protection because it is the will of
God for you. It is in walking out the will of God that your
gifts, anointing, and call operate to the fullest potential.

Each of us has a mantle that fits perfectly. You cannot wear another's mantle and your mantle will not fit anyone else.

An example of this is in David's life when he faced Goliath. He was a teenaged shepherd who knew the power of faith in God. David accepted the challenge of the giant, but King Saul was in fear. Saul was afraid that David would be killed and so gave him his own armor.

> *"Then Saul clothed David with his armor; he put a bronze helmet on his head and clothed him with a coat of mail.*
>
> *And David girded his sword over his armor. Then he tried to go, but could not, for he was not used to it. And David said to Saul, I cannot go with these, for I am not used to them. And David took them off"* (1 Samuel 17: 38,39).

Saul's armor did not fit David. He could not move in someone else's mantle, he could only be successful in his own. David was wise enough to remove it and was able to slay Goliath. David's faith in God not only delivered him that day, but it also altered the future of his entire nation.

Elijah wore his literal mantle while he did great exploits for the Lord. When he was taken up in the chariot of fire, he left his mantle behind for Elisha. That was the mantle of the prophet and Elisha picked it up and did even more in his lifetime than Elijah. While Elijah was alive, however, Elisha did not wear the mantle because it did not belong to him. Elisha did not attempt to walk in Elijah's anointing until the Lord provided for him to do so. The mantle then became his.

Pursue your own mantle and you will have success wearing it. If your mantle is prophetic intercession, then take up that mantle. Know and settle in your heart that you are making a difference and the Body of Christ has need of you. You are special and touch the heart of the Father in a unique way that no one else can replicate. Just as fingerprints are distinctive, we each have an exclusive place in the heart of the Father. Allow His Holy Spirit to move through you, showing others Jesus in you, lifting them up before the Lord in the way that only you can.

Your acts of mercy and your prayers are not overlooked by God.

> *"And when he looked on him, he was afraid, and said, What is it, Lord? And he said unto him, Thy prayers and thine alms are come up for a memorial before God"* (Acts 10:4).

You see, your prayers are like a monument before God. Memorials are markers of special meetings with God. Whenever God visited with the patriarchs in the Old Testament, they would build a memorial of stones to remember the day of visitation. We visit with God every time we take the time for intercessory prayer. Our prayers then become a memorial and God remembers our prayers. We bring His Word before Him and He remembers His promises.

> *"Put Me in remembrance [remind Me of your merits]; let us plead and argue together. Set forth your case, that you may be justified (proved right)"* (Isaiah 43:26 AMP).

Always cherish in your heart the fact that God has set us high upon a Rock and has defended us. That Rock is the Chief Cornerstone, Jesus Christ. Allow Him to be your Savior and the Lord of your life. Let Him be everything He is and you know. Let everything you do open up a door for Him to walk through with you.

As I reflect over the years of my walk with Jesus, He has healed me of so much in my life. He causes my heart to sing even in the midst of a storm. He is my portion and my everything, filling up every area of my life. Jesus has truly given me beauty for ashes.

> *"To appoint unto them that mourn in Zion, to give unto them beauty for ashes, the oil of joy for mourning, the garment of praise for the spirit of heaviness; that they might be called trees of righteousness, the planting of the LORD, that he might be glorified" (Isaiah 61:3).*

My life has not been free from suffering and pain, disappointments and frustrations. However, in all things He causes me to triumph, turning everything that has been meant for my destruction into something good, and He replaces every sorrow with joy in Him.

He has brought life to my bones and a heart that knows what it means to wait on Him.

> *"But they that wait upon the LORD shall renew their strength; they shall mount up with wings as eagles; they shall run, and not be weary; and they shall walk, and not faint" (Isaiah 40:31).*

He is the Rock inside that won't be shaken. All that He has done for me He is willing to do for you, because He is no respecter of persons (Acts 10:34). Jesus is calling you to enter into communion with Him and to follow Him, one step, one day at a time.

Author Contact Information

A Great Love, Inc.

P.O. Box 1248

Toccoa, GA 30577

Phone: (706) 886-5161

Fax: (706) 886-1062

E-mail: ministry@agreatlove.org

Books by Bobbie Jean Merck

The Miracle of Intercession	$2.00
Power of the Secret Place	$10.95
Spoiling Python's Schemes	$11.95
Hope	$9.95
Delay Is Not Denial	$8.95

Books by Dr. Ben Campbell Johnson

The Heart of Paul	$9.95
Matthew and Mark	$9.95
Luke and John	$9.95

Books by Pearl Ballew Jenkins

And He Sent Them Forth	$8.95

To order any of the above books contact the office of A Great Love, Inc.

A Great Love, Inc.
P.O. Box 1248
Toccoa, GA 30577
Phone: (706) 886-5161
Fax: (706) 886-1062
E-mail: ministry@agreatlove.org